Moore, T. E. *Truman*
   The Slaves we rent.

331.670
M

THE SLAVES WE RENT

THE SLAVES
WE RENT

TRUMAN MOORE

Photographs by the Author

RANDOM HOUSE   NEW YORK

Special thanks and acknowledgment to the following for permission to reprint:

Doubleday & Company, Inc.—From *No Other Harvest*, by R. L. Hardman. Copyright © 1962 by R. L. Hardman. Reprinted by permission of Doubleday & Company, Inc.
Houghton Mifflin Company—From *Let Us Now Praise Famous Men*, by James Agee. Copyright 1941 by James Agee & Walker Evans.
Littlefield, Adams & Company—From *American History After 1865*, Fifth Edition, by Ray A. Billington, by permission of Littlefield, Adams & Co., Copyright 1963.
Ludlow Music, Inc.—From "Pastures of Plenty" (song), words and music by Woody Guthrie. © Copyright 1960 & 1963, Ludlow Music, Inc., New York, N. Y. Used by permission.
Twentieth Century Fund—From *Farms and Farmers in an Urban Age*, by Edward Higbee. Twentieth Century Fund, 1963.
The University of Chicago Press—From *Seeds of Southern Change*, by Wilma Dykeman and James Stokely (1962). Reprinted by permission of The University of Chicago Press.
The Viking Press Inc.—From *The Grapes of Wrath*, by John Steinbeck (1939).
Henry Anderson—From *Fields of Bondage* (1962), and to paraphrase excerpts from *To Build a Union* (1963).
Dr. Ernesto Galarza—From *Strangers in Our Fields* (1956).
Bill Mauldin—The cartoon "Plowed Under," © Copyright 1961, by Bill Mauldin.
Carey McWilliams—From *Factories in the Field*.
National Council of Churches—The song "Calling for Migrants."

FIRST PRINTING

© Copyright, 1965, by Truman Moore

Library of Congress Catalog Card Number: 65-11274

MANUFACTURED IN THE UNITED STATES OF AMERICA BY
The Haddon Craftsmen, Inc., Scranton, Pa.

THIS BOOK IS DEDICATED TO

Lyn Terrill

AND

John Ehle

If fields are prisons, where is Liberty?

—Robert Bloomfield,
"The Farmer's Boy"

PREFACE

During a recent campaign, a loudspeaker car blared down
Lexington Avenue in New York City. "Who are the starving
Americans? Where are they? Do you know any?" the car
speaker demanded of the indifferent crowds pushing and
shoving in and out of Grand Central Terminal. No one
seemed to hear these baiting questions. Each hurried along to
his own business with his thoughts undisturbed.

They were good questions. They didn't deserve to be
lost in the roar of traffic.

Yes. There *are* starving Americans. But "starving" is a
cruel word. Even "hungry" is a little harsh. The preferred
euphemism is "undernourished." Or we say "suffer from
malnutrition," "don't get enough to eat," or "go to bed
hungry."

Where are they? In southern Arkansas in early spring
they camp by the fields or live in caves by the river. In California they live in dilapidated shacks scattered among the
broad valleys. In Benton Harbor, Michigan, they crowd at
dawn around the little frame building that houses the Farm
Placement Service.

In Belle Glade, and in many other little towns of the
Florida winter gardens, they gather around the labor buses
to haggle with the "crew leaders" over the day's wages. In

Lubbock, Texas, they work the winter cotton and move on. In Altus, Oklahoma, they live out the bitter winter in frigid tin sheds. In New Jersey, in upstate New York, and on Long Island they crowd into sad hovels on the edges of the fields and into the slums around the towns and cities.

Who are these people living so poorly? What happened to their share of the wealth of America?

The answer lies in the whole story of the migrant worker. It goes back to the middle of the last century. It is not a proud story or a pleasant one to tell.

The migrant today is part of a system—Spanish in origin, and still tinged with the plantation way of life—as out of place in modern America as a slave ship in New York harbor.

Migrant workers are not protected by the basic social legislation most of us take for granted. Being citizens of the United States in general but of no state in particular, they seldom are able to vote. No political machines have risen from their ambulatory slums.

Child labor, that evil of the nineteenth century, still exists in the field. This is not the labor of farm children on vacation, but of migrant children, homeless and schoolless.

Farming, say the big growers, is "different." So different that there is no place in it for workmen's compensation, minimum wages, unemployment insurance, and the right to collective bargaining.

But how is it different? Farming today, on the big commercial farms that grow most of our food and hire most of the migrants, is big business. It is prosperous and profitable. It has never been so good. And the migrants are the underprivileged labor of this overprivileged industry.

Help must come. Perhaps it will—through President Johnson's war on poverty. A reporter from the *New York Times* borrowed a phrase from *Vogue* magazine when he noted that "people are talking about poverty." Economists are redefining it. A family of four with an income of no more than $5,000 a year is "deprived"; on less than $3,000 they are in "abject poverty." (But the average migrant has never made more than $1,000 a year from farm work alone.)

Under the new definition one fifth of the nation's population is poor. They are poor in comparison to those around them. A writer in the *Saturday Evening Post* said of the new poor, "Such a man is poor, statistically. But he is also poor in a far more damaging way: he is a failure in his neighbor's eyes and in his own."

The migrants are not just "statistically" poor. Neither are they statistically hungry or cold. The poverty of the migrant is the old-fashioned kind. It is to be without food, without clothes, without shelter, and without hope in this world.

Without them—these two million men, women, and children who work the fields every year—the rise of American agriculture would not have been possible. If we are to hold up our proud harvests to show the world the fruits of democracy, we can ill afford to maintain this corps of harvesters, who have been called "the slaves we rent."

The migratory labor force in the United States is made up of many different kinds of people. To speak generally about so diverse a group is especially difficult. And in a short book on a broad subject, some generalization is necessary.

I regret that the term "migrant" had to be used. It is an offensive term to those it describes. But I could find no substitute. Unfortunately, a phrase like "itinerant harvester" is a little awkward to use throughout a book. And "seasonal farm worker" is confusing, since a seasonal farm worker might not travel, whereas the migrants do.

The reader who is familiar with migratory work patterns and conditions in his own county or state may find some of the material herein at a variance with his personal observations. But to the best of my knowledge, there are no exceptions that would make what I have written misrepresent the hard realities of life "on the season" as it exists across the nation.

The stories in this book are true, the people are real. But for obvious reasons, many names have had to be changed and individual characteristics altered to conceal actual identity. In some cases the locales have been changed.

I have interviewed migrant workers, crew leaders, growers, union officials, social workers, and many other observers of migrant America. I have traveled thousands of miles across the United States, visiting places where the migrants live and work.

I have relied heavily upon many reports, Senate hearings, studies, articles, and earlier books on seasonal farm labor. (At the end of the book, under the heading "Reading Notes," the reader will find some of the basic sources, as well as some additional material pertinent to each chapter.)

I am greatly indebted to Norman Smith, of the Agricultural Workers Organizing Committee, AFL-CIO; Henry P. Anderson, AWOC's former research director; Dr. Ernesto Galarza; Mrs. M. C. Stone; Miss Faye Bennett, of the National Advisory Committee on Farm Labor; Carey McWilliams, now editor of *The Nation,* and author of two classic studies on migratory labor in the 1930's; Bard McAllister, of the American Friends; Mrs. Katherine Peake, of the Emergency Committee to Aid Farm Workers; Cesar Chavez, of the Farm Workers Association; Eric Thor, of the Giannini Foundation; Betty Spenser, social worker in the Okeechobee Labor Camp; Polly Richards and Georgie Hughes; Cassandra Stockberger, who was a field representative of the National Council of Churches in Arkansas; Frank Rush and the Reverends Jack Mansfield, Earl Kragnes, Wayne Hartmire, Ed Krueger, and Art Jenkens—all of the Migrant Ministry; Leland Duval, farm editor of the Little

Rock *Arkansas Gazette;* and many migratory workers who were either reluctant to give their names, or whose names I have and am reluctant to print.

I would also like to express my appreciation to my wife, who read the manuscript first and typed it. And to Robert Loomis, my editor, for his sympathy, interest, and great patience in editing the manuscript.

CONTENTS

PART ONE

The Stream

1

A MIGRANT PATH
ACROSS AMERICA

It's a mighty hard row that my pore
    hands have hoed,
My pore feet have traveled a hot dusty
    road,
Out of your dustbowl and westward we
    rolled,
Your deserts was hot, and your
    mountains was cold.

I've worked in your orchards of peaches
    and prunes,
I've slept on the ground by the light
    of your moon.
At the edge of your city you will find us
    and then
We come with the dust and we've gone with
    the wind.

FROM "Pastures of Plenty"
WORDS AND MUSIC BY WOODROW WILSON GUTHRIE

THEY MET on a flat vacant lot in Perrine, Florida. They stacked their bundles, boxes, and tattered suitcases by a lone, parched palm tree. They put them there because the tree was the only thing on the lot, and so it seemed natural that it should be the center of the group.

Little Jim said he'd be there with the motor running. No one believed he'd be on time, but just the same they all came early.

It was the last week of April. The morning coolness was brief. Already the low frame buildings across the road had pulled back their shadows, leaving the dust-and-gravel lot to the open sky. By nine o'clock the sun was a hot hazy glare. By ten, the mist had burned away and the sun was a brilliant white dot. It looked like an early summer.

The long wait began. There were forty people now, all Negro—twenty-six men, nine women, two young boys, and three babies. Two of the women were pregnant.

Each woman wore a variation of the same outfit: a bandanna and over this a large straw hat, an oversized man's shirt tucked into a brightly colored full skirt and under this a pair of long pants rolled up to just above the ankles. The knees were reinforced with a section cut from an inner tube. The long sleeves and the high collars protected them from the sun, and the straw hats kept their eyes shaded and prevented the sun from beating down directly on their heads. The bandanna covered the back of the neck. They wore long pants to keep the pesticides off their legs and long sleeves to protect their arms. The rubber tube padded their knees when they knelt down between the rows on the hard ground.

The men wore long shirts and wool hats—tattered, dirty, and ill fitting. A stranger seeing this crew in their field clothes would have taken them to be part of some tribe or clan, for in their strange clothing they did not look like ordinary people. But few of them were friends. They had come to Perrine from all over the South. Most of them had just finished the winter harvests in southern Florida. Now with the coming of summer it was time to move on to the fields of the North. By the time the crew broke up in October, it would have been together a long time.

The sun climbed higher, and the heat rose shimmering from the white ground. The crew moved restlessly about the lot. The babies had started a complaining cry.

Rosie Wilson watched the impatient women. She was tired of waiting, but she was not anxious to get started. She had been up the road too many times. She grew up in the field and expected to die there. It was a bitter and hard life. But she had settled with the world as best she could. Her bitterness had passed with her youth. She no longer hated the world for her misery, but she didn't love it either. She seldom laughed or cried. To the world Rosie turned a vacant and detached expression. She went along. She did what she could. Up the road with a crew, because that's the way it had always been as far back as she could remember.

She liked her corncob pipe, and a pint of muscatel when she could get it. The other women called her "Mammy" when she smoked her pipe. She ignored them or just told them to go to hell. Rosie was a long time past caring what people thought.

It was not impatience that made Flora Benton restless. It was a bad morning for her. The sun made her dizzy. When the ground swayed under her feet she felt panicky. She was a tall, strong woman with smooth, carbon-black skin. She was eight months gone, but perhaps because of her height or her size she looked like five months at most.

Her husband had left her. But as long as her hands were fast and her back was sound and strong, she could pick enough in a day to earn for herself and the child. Weakness and sickness terrified her. She watched the old woman with the pipe. The old woman must have been strong, too. She was still tough, you could tell that. She could take care of herself.

Johnny Brown was one of the young boys in the crew. He and his brother and his mother had been on the season for the past five years, ever since they left Georgia. His father had gone out one Saturday night and was never seen again. He just vanished. The family moved to Florida after they had decided the old man wasn't coming back. Johnny liked it better than south Georgia. He missed a year of school in the move, but he started again in Belle Glade. Each year he missed the last part of the school year and the first three or four weeks of the beginning of the next, because of the crew. Once he was held back a year, but the teachers usually gave him some extra homework, and he would make his grade with the class.

This past year he had been a senior. When his mother told him they were going to the eastern shore with Little Jim's crew, he knew it meant he wouldn't graduate. He tried to get the migrant minister to talk to her, but it was no good. The "Rev" even offered to put him up until school was out and pay his bus fare to Cape Charles. "It ain't the bus fare," she had told him. "It's the money that boy can make every day. We need every nickel we can get."

High school graduate. "Baby, I ain't spending my life in no bean field," he said. One of the men laughed out, "What you gonna do, be President?" He walked aimlessly around the lot, kicking at the gravel.

There is a standing joke in the South that you can tell a man's age by the President he was named after. Theodore Roosevelt Jones was sixty. He had lost his farm during the late thirties. Since then he had been a migrant. Each year the old man got slower. He had a hard time this year getting

Little Jim to put him on. There was nothing for him in Perrine. His wife had left him the year after he lost the farm, and his sons had both gone into the Army. One of them was living in Harlem. He still carried a dog-eared letter his son had written him eight years before. It was the last he had heard from any of them. Once every year or so he would get someone to read the letter to him. There was a part in it where his son told him how much money he was making in the city, and how, pretty soon, he would be able to send a regular check so the old man wouldn't have to work.

It was a ritual with Theodore to look for mail, but he had really given up hoping a long time ago.

Willie Lee Stalvey looked quite a bit like Theodore; also, their lives had been similar. Willie Lee had gone on the season about the same time, for the same reasons. His family had fallen apart, and Willie Lee took to the harvest fields like some men take to drink. Each year he was hoping that the crew would go to a strange new place, but each year the fields looked alike, the camps were the same shacktowns wherever they went.

At noon the crew leader's wife drove up with their car and trailer. A few minutes later the truck came. It was not until late in the afternoon that the crew leader showed up with the bus. He had been to Miami and Homestead looking for more workers, but Little Jim didn't tell the crew that. He told them he had had some work done on the bus, because if they suspected he was having trouble rounding up a crew, they might think he was not as fair and square as he bragged he was.

They loaded their baggage onto the truck—the shabby bundles that held all their worldly goods. Fifteen rode in the truck, and they used cement blocks and potato crates for seats. Beds would be fashioned out of the softer bundles.

The bus was painted baby-blue, interior-flat. Little Jim

had bought the paint cheap at a hardware sale, and had done the job himself, with a stiff brush that left a pattern of marks in the paint deep enough to cast shadows in the evening sun. Carefully lettered in yellow enamel was his name: LITTLE JIM JAMES. The rear door, held shut with rusty wire, bore the parting message: GONE BUT NOT FORGOTTEN. And beneath, a consolation: JESUS LOVES YOU. Around on the side, in the same bright yellow, was the name of the bus: THE BEANPICKER SPECIAL. On the same night the bus was painted, Little Jim's cousin had lettered the name on the side and had insisted that the Beanpicker Special be christened. They celebrated by drinking a bottle of gin, and the cousin explained how he had seen the English queen in a newsreel breaking a bottle against a ship. He seized the empty gin bottle and christened the Beanpicker, breaking one of the front signal lights.

Little Jim was a wiry, nervous man who had a politician's skill at evasion. He answered every question with the standard phrase: "That's right." The questioner always had the feeling he was being agreed with. Little Jim spoke the rapid-fire dialect of his native Pawleys Island, near Georgetown, South Carolina. If pressed too hard, Little Jim could become completely incomprehensible. It was this asset that enabled him to continue as a crew leader. Neither the migrants nor the growers were ever certain of what arrangements they had made with Little Jim, who only made his preference for verbal agreements perfectly clear.

One bus, one truck, one car, one trailer. The caravan, now complete, moved out onto Highway A1A. Little Jim stopped at Pompano, Delray, and Fort Pierce and found ten more workers. There were now thirty-two in the bus, including Johnny Brown and his brother, and the babies.

The trip up the coast was not too eventful.

Once they stopped at a diner, and the man told them to move on. When they stopped for gas, the station attendant wouldn't let them use the rest rooms, so they stopped in the woods. Billboards offered Stuckey's pecan candy with relentless persistence. It was long past midnight when the bus neared the Georgia line. A light fog was closing in on the Beanpicker. The bus driver became aware that the truck and Little Jim's car were not behind him. He pulled off the road and waited, but they did not come. He turned around and drove back for a few miles, stopping at a small filling station. The driver called the sheriff's office, and the highway patrol found the crew leader and the truck driver repairing a flat tire. The bus waited nearly four hours.

They slept, some in the bus, some on the roadside. The babies cried, and there was only warm soda to quiet them.

Some of the crew had brought food: sandwiches, potted meat, and crackers. Others who had joined the crew only at the last moment were without either food or money. They would have to wait until Little Jim was ready to feed them.

In the early morning the caravan resumed the trip. By midmorning the bald tires of the Beanpicker sang on the melting asphalt, and the big produce trucks were pounding past, rocking the bus in their wake. The diesel fumes were added to the stifling heat, making the air unpleasant, and it was difficult to breathe.

They made another bathroom stop near a lonely grove of slash pine. There was an awkward moment as they got off the bus when a carload of tourists stopped and wanted to take pictures. The tourists thought they were going to work in a nearby field. Little Jim started to move on when a man with sunglasses and a camera spotted Rosie with her straw hat and pipe. She posed for him, smilingly accepted the dollar he gave her.

"Make a fool of yo'self," said Johnny Brown.

"Go to hell," said Rosie and stuffed the bill down the front of her dress.

Willie Lee ate the small lunch he had brought with him when he joined the crew. In the week before he left Perrine, all he could find was bean scrapping, and there was not much of that. It took all the money he made to pay for his room and meals. He fought the thoughts of food that lodged in his mind. All night he had dreamed of food.

Late in the evening of that day Little Jim, over his wife's objections, bought some food for the crew. He gave each person a pint of beans, two slices of bread, and a slice of sausage.

Willie Lee tried to bring back the dream about a mountain of food by telling Theodore Roosevelt about it. But it was gone forever. An hour after he had eaten the sausage and beans, he was as hungry as he had been that morning.

As the bus passed through the Carolina low country, it was almost alone on the dark highway. The chirping and croaking of a million frogs was so dense that the bus seemed to be standing still. The nocturnal chorus was lulling, and the swaying bus rocked like a cradle from side to side.

Flora Benton had felt the first rhythmic pains before they left Georgia. Now, in the deep Carolina night, the pounding within her became more persistent. She cried out.

Rosie got to her first. "I thought so," she said. "That's what I thought that girl was going to do." She and Willie Lee lifted the writhing woman into the aisle. Theodore Roosevelt spread out his jacket and went through the bus getting coats and sweaters to pad the iron floor. The driver pulled off the highway near a closed filling station.

When the first golden-gray clouds bounced back to earth the light of the coming sun, life on the Beanpicker had been increased by one.

Flora turned to Rosie and started talking. She talked about the child as if she was thinking out loud. She had wanted the baby to be born in New Jersey. She had thought she could hold out. She wanted him to be born up north in a hospital. But here he was, born on a trip. Maybe that meant he'd go someplace and not be tied to the sack and the hamper. At least he wasn't born at the end of a row of beans like her sister's first boy. And she had him now. They'd be together, the two of them. He would grow to be strong, and he'd be educated. He would look after her when she was too old to go to the fields.

At the edge of every town she looked at people rocking on their porches, watching the old bus go past. She wanted a place where you didn't have to move. Then she could watch people going by instead of always riding past somebody else's porch and seeing them sitting there. She could hang up her clothes in a closet, unpack all her bags and bundles. "If I had a place like that," she said, "I wouldn't go ten foot from the door. All this movin round makes a body old."

Flora clung to her child and gritted her teeth against the jarring of the seat. Theodore Roosevelt had collected everything soft, from old clothes to burlap bags, and had made a nestlike bed in the back of the bus. He had thought of the truck, but it bounced even more than the bus. He asked Little Jim about getting Flora into the trailer, but Little Jim's wife objected.

They stopped several times in South Carolina for minor repairs. The state police trailed the convoy. Flora was thankful for the poor condition of the bus. Just as she was ready to scream, the radiator would boil over and the Beanpicker would stop. The old woman stayed with her, placidly smoking the corncob pipe, which had not gone out since the child was born.

As they neared Fayetteville, in North Carolina, one of the ever-present patrol cars came to life with a wailing siren. With inborn dread of the white laws, the crew awaited its fate.

Neither the truck nor the bus had inspection stickers, or signal lights or horns that worked. Repairs were to be made at once. Little Jim assured the patrolman that he was right, posted a fifteen-dollar bond, and drove on.

Outside Fayetteville they were hauled down at a filling station by another patrolman. The mechanic at the station gave a cost estimate of forty dollars. It was late. The crew had been on the road for three days and two nights. They were tired, hungry, and all for having the work done as soon as possible. But Little Jim refused to pay. He thought the cost was too high and wanted to look for a better price. His two drivers were carted off to jail, and Little Jim started looking.

He drove to the Negro section in Fayetteville and found a place to buy the necessary parts for ten dollars. The man who sold him these was going off duty and couldn't install them, but had a friend who would. Little Jim drove to the man's house, got him out of bed, and got the repairs made.

While the crew waited in the bus, a woman who lived nearby sent over some milk and sandwiches. A few of the workers who had some money paid her. The rest she gave in honor of the infant. The other babies had their first milk since the trip began.

Fayetteville is still remembered by the East Coast migrants as the place where twenty-two were killed when a potato-laden trailer-truck plowed into a truckload of workers. Flora's brother died in that wreck. "Pulled directly into the path of an oncoming trailer-truck" was what the newspapers had said, and she still remembered it that way. Whenever the Beanpicker came to a junction, Flora automatically looked up the highway and thought of "oncoming trucks."

There were four women and a six-month-old baby among the dead. It was in all the newspapers, and everybody said something would be done about the way they had to travel. But the only thing that happened was that the patrol always gave you a ticket now.

At eight o'clock the next morning the two drivers were retrieved from the jailhouse. It was the morning of the fourth day. Little Jim was busted. He wired the grower for money and picked it up at Wilson.

They drove straight through, stopping only for gas. The highway patrol kept a close vigilance on the bus. Late in the evening they arrived at their destination, over a thousand miles from Perrine. The trip had taken four days and four nights with stops for repairs—or jail—on an average of every fifty miles.

The camp, a dismal group of twelve cabins, was lit by a flickering kerosene lantern in the yard. It offered the crew of the Beanpicker an empty welcome. The truck was unloaded, and most of the crew members went off to find their cabins. A lone man sat slumped over by the window in the back of the bus. "He's sleeping off his wine," said Little Jim. But someone said it was Theodore Roosevelt, and Theodore didn't drink. When they tried to wake him, they saw that he was dead. They carried him into an end cabin that stood off by itself. He was an old man, and he died the way old men should. Quietly, in the dark of the night. In the morning they would call the preacher.

Johnny Brown told his mother he was going to help Little Jim. He ran through the camp yard, circling around where the lantern burned. He cut through the woods, and without looking back, headed for the highway.

The trip was over, the first part at least. In another month they would start out for New Jersey. In three days the crop would be in, and there would be work. The year before, Little Jim's crew had waited almost two weeks before there was work. By that time Little Jim owned their souls.

In the early spring there is a pause just before the migrants hit the road. This is the time when the rush on the crops begins. It is a time of getting packed, getting crews together, and then the race is on. There are times when field after field is in harvest, and it seems that China herself could not satisfy the demand for hands to pick the crop and speed it to the distant markets before the price drops. And then all of a sudden a man can go a thousand miles and find no work.

The Beanpicker was only one bus carrying one crew. Each year when the harvest begins, thousands of buses like this haul thousands of crews to fields across America as millions of migrant workers hit the road.

They go in crews like Little Jim's, riding flat-bed trucks or condemned school buses patched together for just one more season. They go by car—Hudson bombers, engines knocking, laying a smoke screen of oil. They go in prewar Fords, packed with bags, bundles, pots and pans, children crying. They go in pickups made into mobile tents—a home for the season. They ride the rods of the "friendly" Southern Pacific.

From rural Mexico they come on bare feet, walking by day, sleeping in the bushes by night, headed for the big reception centers along the border. From San Juan they come by jet. They come from the West Indies, from Japan, from Canada, from lost farms in the Black Belt, from closed mines in the mountains of Kentucky and West Virginia.

They come from wherever men are desperate for work. They come by whatever means they can find. These are the migrants—the Gasoline Gypsies, the Rubber Tramps—crossing and recrossing America, scouring the countryside in a land where the season never ends. There's always a harvest somewhere. From Florida to Oregon, the fruit tramp pursues the orchards. From Texas to Michigan, the berry migrants work from field to field. Each year two million men, women, and children invade every state but one to pick fruit, to chop cotton, to scrap beans, to top onions, to bunch carrots, to pull corn, to fill their hampers with the richest harvest earth ever yielded to man.

The circus and the college beach parties leave Florida

after Easter. By the first week in April the major league clubs wind up their spring training and go home to play ball. The "snowbirds" start back to the cities of the North with their tans. And the migrants go up the road on the season. The spring harvests begin while snow covers much of the nation. When the winter crops are in, the migrants form crews and follow the sun. Sometimes a single bus will carry a crew; sometimes they pass in ragged convoys as the migrant battalions rumble out of Florida and up the eastern seaboard.

The full invasion of migrants hits South Carolina in May, North Carolina and Virginia by June. By late summer they have passed through Pennsylvania into New Jersey and New York State. Some go into Delaware and Maryland, others to Long Island, and a few on to Maine. By October the up-state crops are in and the migrant tide ebbs back to the southern tip of Florida.

They find little work in November. It is after a lean Thanksgiving and a bleak Christmas that hands are needed again in the fields and groves of the winter gardens.

From Texas the pattern is much the same. This is the home base of the largest migrant stream. The exodus begins in early spring. The Mexico Mexicans move in and the Texas Mexicans move out. Storekeepers close down for the season as the little towns depopulate. Everyone who can bend and stoop starts for the great corporate farms of the North and the West.

From the torrid valleys of Arizona and California to the great Pacific Northwest, there is a string of harvests. There is no crop in the world that can't be grown on the Pacific Coast, and relatively few that aren't. What was once a vast desert wasteland is now rich irrigated valleys, principally the Imperial and the San Joaquin. In constant sunshine and several inches of water, crop after crop is produced with factorylike precision.

Into all these fields, through state after state, the migrants

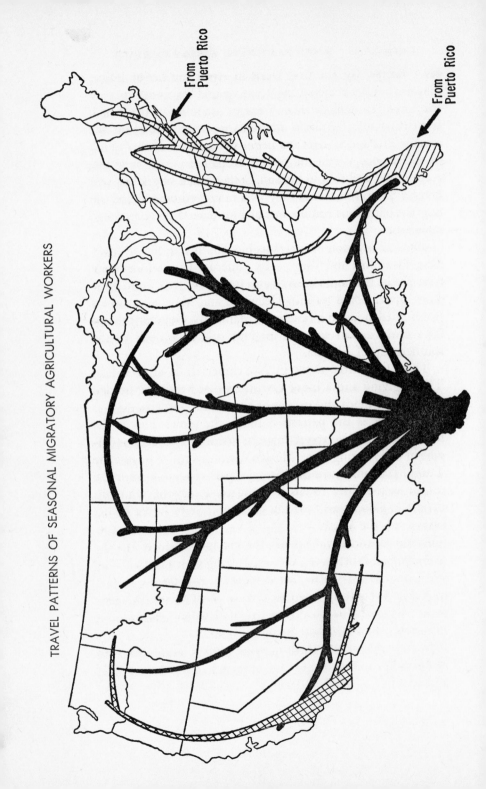

TRAVEL PATTERNS OF SEASONAL MIGRATORY AGRICULTURAL WORKERS

From Puerto Rico

From Puerto Rico

cut a footpath across America. But in spite of their mobility, they are confined within their own world. Migrant America is a network of side roads, of farm towns and labor camps and river banks, of fields and packing sheds. The cities important to them are not New York, Boston, and San Francisco, but the capitals of the agricultural empire of the big growers: Homestead, Riverhead, Belle Glade, Stockton, and Benton Harbor. For the migrant, no roadside motel or tavern offers a blinking-neon welcome. No host community sees them as a potential source of revenue but as a blight on the community's health and a threat to the relief rolls. Businessmen, dance bands, and tourists making their way across the country find many services and comforts at their disposal. The migrant can hope for good weather, a grassy bank, and a filling station that will permit him to use the rest room. A warm bed and a hot meal are still a long way from St. Louis.

There is always blood on the harvest moon. No one knows how many luckless migrants have been slaughtered on their way to gather in the harvest.

Traveling on the nation's highways is dangerous enough with a sound vehicle and a good driver. But it is doubly dangerous for migrants, who are hauled about in flat-bed trucks and condemned school buses retrieved from the junk yard to begin a new life on the season. The hazards of faulty brakes, worn-out tires, poor lights, and mechanical malfunctions are compounded by drivers who are fatigued, drunk, or incompetent. Overcrowding, which causes blocked exits and jammed aisles, often turns highway accidents into real tragedies. It was not until 1965 that the Federal Government required crew leaders to carry liability insurance on farm workers while they are on the road.

In 1963 there were three migrant crashes loud enough to be heard beyond the fields. One of them happened in Florida, and two in California.

The Florida wreck occurred in the heart of the citrus belt. Lake Okeechobee is immediately visible on a map of Florida as a large hole in the southern tip. But a motorist can drive past the lake and not see it at all. The lake is rimmed by embankments, and its water fed into canals. Along the banks of Lake Okeechobee is Clewiston, a company town dominated by the U. S. Sugar Corporation; Belle Glade, a capital of the migrant world; and Pahokee, another migrant center. The Hillsboro Canal starts just above Belle Glade and runs toward the Atlantic through Palm Beach County for fifty miles, ending on the coast at Boca Raton, midway between Palm Beach and Miami. State Road 827 runs alongside the canal as far as Shawano Plantation, where the road ends. This road is straight and narrow. On May 18, 1963, a Negro called Poor Boy Slim had forty-two workers aboard his bus. A truck driven by a white man started to pass Poor Boy Slim's bus, just outside Belle Glade. The bumpers hooked together. There was a brief moment of terror. Some of the passengers on the packed bus saw what was happening. Others never knew. The bus plunged into the waters of the Hillsboro Canal and sank. Twenty-seven harvesters drowned in the canal. Twelve of them were children who should have been in school.

The whites in Belle Glade stood solidly behind the truck driver before many of them knew the details of the accident. They blamed Poor Boy Slim for the mass drowning and deplored the return of the glare of national publicity first created by the *CBS Reports* documentary "Harvest of Shame," which was partly filmed in Belle Glade.

For a week there were two to seven funerals a day, the last on Sunday. A memorial service was held in the Belle Glade Armory. For a few days afterward, no one wanted to ride the labor buses. But there was no other way to get to work. Belle Glade returned to normal.

Not long after this, on September 18, a busload of sixty-

three Mexican field workers approached a small grade crossing near Chualar, California, about eight miles south of
Salinas. The bus was returning from a celery field to the
Earl Meyers Company labor camp. Just as the bus was crossing the tracks, the driver heard the sickening scream of a
train whistle. A few seconds later a Southern Pacific freight,
pulling seventy sugar-beet gondola cars, plowed into the
bus.

It took a half mile for the train to stop. The front of the
engine was plastered with sheet metal and mangled bodies,
the remains of the makeshift bus and its crew. Behind the
train lay a line of dying men, shoes, hats, and cutting knives.
A lettuce worker in a nearby field said, "Bodies just flew
all over the place."

Twenty-two men died that afternoon by the tracks.
Within a few hours six more died in Monterey County
Hospital. The death toll finally climbed to thirty-two. It
was the worst accident in California's history. The governor
promised "a complete investigation."

Eleven days later in Westmoreland, California, at the foot
of Superstition Mountain in the Imperial Valley, another
bus of migrants plunged into a drainage canal. All thirty-
nine were injured, four seriously.

The harvest sacrifice is not always made in great numbers.
A few years ago a half-ton truck left Texas for the sugar-
beet fields of Wyoming. In it were fifty-four migrant workers. As the truck neared the outskirts of Agate, Colorado,
the driver suddenly hit the brakes. The truck spun around
and turned over twice, scattering workers across the highway. There was one death: a baby who died in a Denver
hospital shortly after the accident. (Someone asked the
driver why he stepped on the brakes. He said he didn't
remember.)

In the same state not long after this, a truck carried
twenty-six workers through a heavy storm. When it finally

stopped to give the people some air (the windows were closed tight as protection against the rain), a six-month-old baby had suffocated.

During October of 1963, not three miles from the scene of the Fayetteville massacre where the truckload of migrants died in 1957, a truck carrying twenty-four bean pickers turned over when a tire blew out, scattering its human cargo like a handful of oats. Fortunately no one was killed.

The National Safety Council urges: "Buckle your seat belts." The plea is certainly not aimed at the migrant worker astride a potato crate in the back of a flat-bed truck. "Stay awake" urge the big green signs on the interstate highways, apparently not intended for crew leaders. Fifteen migrants were killed in an Arizona crash when the exhausted driver fell asleep at the wheel. Those killed were asleep on the floor of the canvas-covered truck.

When the Interstate Commerce Commission was considering regulation on migrant transportation in 1957, a representative of the "jolly" Green Giant Company complained that restriction on travel between 8 P.M. and 6 A.M. was a hardship on the workers and on the employers. "It has been our experience," said the company's spokesman, "that these trucks can complete the trip from Texas to Wisconsin in from fifty to sixty hours with stops only for meals, gasoline, and general stretching . . ."

A vegetable packer said it was practically impossible to attach seats securely and still use the trucks to haul produce. Amazingly enough, he did not use this as an argument against carrying workers in produce trucks but against using seats.

Many crew leaders use trucks because of the extra money they can make hauling the crops from the fields to the processors. Jon Misner, the director of migrant labor at Stokely-Van Camp in Indianapolis, said he knew crew leaders who made $15,000 hauling vegetables—in an eight-week season.

Since the average migrant earns only about $1,000 a year, many wonder why they go on the season at all. The answer can be made complicated or it can be kept simple. The longer answer would consider the decline of the tenant farm, racial discrimination, automation, and active recruitment by crew leaders, the Farm Placement Service, and the big growers.

Children who grow up in the migrant camps have little education or contact with the urban world. They are migrants by birth and have little choice in the matter. Some workers use the migrant stream as an escape. A New York State man, following the crops in the West, said he left home because he couldn't stand his wife. He walked out one night thirty years ago and hasn't been east of the Mississippi since.

The simple answer is probably nearer the truth in most cases. A man goes on the season when he's busted. He takes it as his last chance.

Will Rogers said that America was the first nation to go to the poorhouse in an automobile. It is still the only nation with a motorized peasant class living in a kind of floating slum that touches the outskirts of the biggest cities and crosses every state. Travel in America, migrant-style, is a grinding ordeal. The affluence on all sides only makes the poverty of the migrant more conspicuous and more unbearable.

The Brent family is typical of many thousands of migrant families who have blundered into the migrant stream. They were forced off their land in Georgia when the owner combined it with five other "mule and nigger" farms. One afternoon a placard appeared in the window of the filling station/grocery store near their home. It offered "employment opportunities" at the harvest in Homestead, Florida. The family was desperate for work. They loaded their household goods into their 1940 Dodge and started for Homestead.

After a long, hot, and dusty trip, they stopped in Belle Glade, north of Homestead, where the harvest was under way. Once there, they found plenty of work, and the whole family went to the fields. In a month it was all over. They never got to Homestead. Work was finished there, too.

They realized, too late, that they would have to go where the crops were. They sold their car and joined a crew headed for Pennsylvania. They had become migrants.

Many families know people who are on the season, and have heard what it's like. But when their luck runs out they join a crew anyway. It's pick beans or starve.

Crew leaders and roving bus drivers make recruiting trips into the South, and many workers enter the stream this way. The promise of "a hundred dollars a week and living in a ho-tel" sounds good. A favorite target of the recruiters is the debt-ridden tenant family. Cash earnings and a place to live are heady inducements.

The lure of good money and travel attracts high school boys like George and Frank Smith. They were recruited from their home town in South Carolina. Both were just out of school and could find no work. When the labor bus came through they boarded it with misgivings, but it was the only job they could find.

Once on the season, it quickly became apparent that as migrant harvesters they would have to work hard and fast just to make ends meet, even in the best of times. Between harvests they had to struggle for a bare existence. They made trips to Utica when the crew was working in upstate New York, and later to Baltimore, to look for regular work, but they found nothing. When the crew returned to Florida, George and Frank had to go with it. Like many other migrants, they found themselves trapped in the stream.

Some families enter the stream to search for a better place to live. One member will go on the season to look around up north or out west. Still, many of them wind up in the rural slums that lie on the fringes of the suburbs across the land.

There are, for example, many Negroes from North Carolina living in Riverhead, Long Island. They came with migrant crews first, and later returned with their families. It is a slow and difficult process. A Long Island woman explained it this way: "A man comes alone with a crew and picks a place to settle down. The next season he may come back with one of the men in the family. If they decide it's okay, he'll come the following year with his wife. At the end of the season they stay in Riverhead. No one wants to hire a migrant, because they're supposed to be wild and unstable, nor rent him a house for fear he'll tear it up. So the first place the family lives in is a real chicken house. If he finds a job, he can move his family out of the ex-migrant slum into a regular slum. After that, he's got it made. A lot of them don't, and they get stranded. Sometimes the husband has to leave so the wife can get welfare."

The valleys of California and Arizona and the suburbs of the Middle West are filled with the cabin slums of Mexican-Americans, Negroes, and poor whites trying to settle down.

After a few years a migrant who does not or cannot escape the stream is broken by it. The poverty, anxiety, homelessness, and isolation wear away his spirit. It is this apathy and loss of hope that is often called acceptance ("They like things that way").

"We're always goin someplace," said a sandy-haired Oklahoma migrant, "but we never git noplace." In a tired flat voice, an old woman in a Michigan field put it only a little differently: "I been everplace, and I got noplace."

A migrant minister in a Belle Glade camp asked a woman in his camp church if she was going on the season again. "I don't know," she answered. "Ever year I go up broke, and I come back broke. I don't know why I go, even."

A migrant in Arkansas sat on the steps of his one-room cabin. For an hour he had talked about where he had been and the things he had done to keep his family alive. Suddenly it seemed as if the memory of the years crushed him. "I get sick of the world sometimes and everbody in it. Used to make a livin pickin cotton. Then they started bringin in them Mexicans by the truckload. And now they're gettin them machines. I don't know what's goin to happen."

Few urban Americans have any concept of this vast impoverished army that tramps through their country to bring the crops in from the fields. It shows itself to the urban world only as a broken-down car or bus here, a truck there, a ragged crew working somewhere off in a field.

2

THE CREW LEADER

The bus was army surplus, a 1942 dirt-brown GMC with broken windows and bald tires. The fenders were hung together by patch weld, and it had the name Martinez painted on each side in crude blue letters . . .

He'd stand at the bus door chanting until it was loaded: "Good cotton, easy pickin'. No gleanin', first of the field. Twenty-five and we go. Come on! Fog's liftin'. Come on! Twenty-five and she rolls!"

—R. L. HARDMAN, *No Other Harvest*

LITTLE JIM was a good crew leader. His bus, the Bean-picker Special, was a little run-down, and the tires were slick. But the driver was sober and careful.

The camps that Little Jim found for his crew while they were on the road were not always what he had promised them, but he could hardly help that. He couldn't demand that the grower put the crew up in the Holiday Inn. But he refused to deal with a couple of growers who were notorious for their pigsty camps.

The crew went hungry before the crop came in, but Little Jim had never told them he was going to feed them. If he lent them money to buy food before they got work, he charged them no more than the going rates, just like a bank.

And he was not greedy about the money he took from their pay. A dime out of every dollar was his take. He stuck to it. And he charged them a couple of dollars for each job he got them, which was no more than three or four a season. And while they were on the road, he got them to "help on the gas."

When he took out money for Social Security, he always turned it in, as he was supposed to.

If there was a big shopping center on the way back from the field, he'd stop and let the crew do their shopping there instead of in the little stores near the camp, where they always overcharged.

His wife thought he was stupid to pass up any chance to make money. He'd give in to her now and then. So he sold moonshine. There was a good profit in that. "I keep a little around because some of them—they won't work without it. If you don't have it for them, they'll go out and get it." He bought it from a bootlegger for $1 a quart, and sold it in the fields at 50 cents a shot. A heavy drinker gets thirsty in the field. But Little Jim had to be careful and not give a bad drinker too much. He had one worker who was a mean drunk. He pulled out a homemade machete one afternoon and almost took a man's head off. After that Little Jim was more careful.

He was usually on the road with the crew four to five months a year. During that time, he was the crew's official representative. It is the crew leader, not the grower or the corporate farm, who is recognized as the employer. Whether or not a migrant ends the season money ahead or money behind often depends on his crew leader. Little Jim's crew was lucky he was honest.

But not all crew leaders are like Little Jim. There are over 8,000 crew leaders in the migrant streams. They come in all shades of reliability and honesty. Good or bad, the crew leaders perform a service that is invaluable to the grower. For example, a farmer can make a simple agreement with a crew leader for a given number of migrants at a specified date. They will agree on a price, and the farmer, theoretically, can rest assured that his labor problems will be taken care of. In practice, however, the farmer can never rest easy until he sees the crew pull into camp. An unscrupulous crew leader can shift his crew to a higher-paying farm at the last minute. The first farmer can easily lose his crop for lack of a harvest crew.

Because both the migrants and the farmers depend on the crew leader, he is in a good position to take advantage of both. Hamilton Daniels was like that.

You had to admire Hamp. He was a thorough professional, with imagination and style. He usually honored his obligations to deliver the promised number of workers at the agreed price and time. Sometimes he came a little late, though, because he would stop for a few small unscheduled jobs on the way.

Hamp was born in New Orleans,. A diplomat and a shrewd judge of character, Hamp had a grasp of things far beyond what five years in school had given him. He knew how to get along with the white growers. He just played Uncle Tom.

Sometimes, when the grower was around, Hamp would ride herd on the crew just to let the man know he was in charge. But the growers knew that. They depended on Hamp to bring the migrants in on time and get them out when the work was done. Neither Hamp nor the grower would profit by argument. His dealings with the growers were usually cordial, if strained. A balance of power existed that neither cared to test.

He negotiated a price with each grower, but arrangements were standard, since many growers get together before the season and agree on what they will pay.

Hamp could take a flat price for harvesting. When he did this, it meant he would have to ride the crew hard. Then he'd have to cut their pay as low as they'd stand for.

On a flat-fee basis, Hamp's profit was the difference between what the grower paid him and what he paid the crew. Hamp didn't care for this because if the weather was too hot or it rained too much, Hamp might even *lose* money.

The grower might agree to an hourly rate for picking, but this was rare. If there was a good crop and a high market, the grower might agree to an hourly rate so the crew would take their time and not damage the crop.

But the usual arrangement was a piece rate. This fixed the cost for Hamp and the grower. The rates were usually set up on a sliding scale. When the crop was good, the rates were lower. And as the fields thinned out, the rates went up. This is when the "bonus" system was used. When the fields thinned out, the crew didn't want to work it because it was hard to make any money. The grower would pay a bonus at the end of the harvest to all the workers who stayed on the job. But it really wasn't a bonus. He just withheld some of their money until the job was finished.

Whatever arrangement was made, the crew seldom knew the details. If the grower made his camp rent-free as part of the payment, Hamp might still charge the crew rent. He was careful never to cut into a man's pay directly, except to take out Social Security—which he never turned in.

His dealings with the migrant crew were complex. For one thing, he lived closely with them. The impression he made on them was important. If a crew leader looked too prosperous, the crew might think he was crooked. If he looked too poor, they might doubt he was a good crew leader. Hamp managed to look just right. He wore a pair of brown pants and a red shirt which were ragged to the point of fascination. He was the raggediest man they'd ever seen. Close examination of this costume would have revealed patches sewn over whole cloth, but the effect was one of arresting poverty. As a contrast to this, Hamp drove a Cadillac. His garments attested to his humility, and his car to his success.

In picking a crew, Hamp seemed to work with little thought or design. Actually he was very careful about whom he took on. He wouldn't take boys who looked as if they were trying to save money for college in the fall. They held on too tight to their money. And most of them would leave the crew to start school before the season was over.

Hamp looked for the quirk. The twist. The reason this man or woman wanted to work the crops. He preferred workers, either male or female, in the first stages of alcoholism. Some crew leaders wouldn't hire the drinkers, but Hamp knew better. You had to wait until a man was hooked. Then he didn't seem to know or care what you took out of his pay as long as he had enough to eat and drink. They might get mad. But they didn't go far. Of course, a hardened wino was worthless. He couldn't stand the pace. It isn't easy to bend over in the broiling sun all day.

Hamp kept a good supply of "white mule," and had places along the way where he could get it. There was good money in it. He also kept little white packets of dope. There was the real money. But sometimes it was hard to get. You really had to push it all the time to make it pay. And it was too bad if the government men caught you with "junk."

Hamp decided it was too much of a risk. And it took a lot of time. So he let the pushers into the camp, and charged them a cut of what they made. That was the trouble with pushing, anyway—everybody got a cut. He might as well get his. And he did keep a few packets in the camp if a man should need it badly.

He also kept his hand in the ordinary rackets. He got a 15 percent cut from the grocery store near the camp. The store would raise the prices to the workers. If the storekeeper refused to pay a kickback, Hamp would take the crew to another store. The crew seldom had cash, so Hamp worked out a credit system with the storekeeper. The crew members were never shown an itemized bill; they just paid what Hamp said they owed.

Hamp also kept a supply of beer and cigarettes in his trailer at double the store prices. And for a 50-cent bottle of wine, he charged $1.45. None of the crew stocked up on these things because they never had the cash.

A few years ago Hamp took two prostitutes along in the crew, although he usually relied on camp followers. Either way, he got his share of what they made. Between the bad years and the good, the price ran from three to five dollars. Hamp let the women make enough to keep them happy. He taxed their excess profits. If you cut a whore's profits too close, she got indiscriminate and tried to make it up on volume. Then VD was sure to run through the camp. However, a couple of prostitutes were good for morale, even if business was bad and brought in little money.

With his various sidelines, Hamp made almost as much money as he did on the actual harvest.

With one thing and another, Hamp cleared about $20,-000 during a fair year. Some of it he spent on his own pleasures, some he put in the bank or in his store in Florida. And every few years he bought another second-hand bus for the crew.

Crooked as he was, Hamp lacked the cruelty of some crew leaders. Willard Barnes had a crew in a Long Island camp working in potatoes. When the time came for them to go South, one old woman in the crew was too sick to travel. Willard put off the trip for two days, but the old woman didn't get any better. So he just packed up the crew and left her. She awoke from a feverish sleep and saw the first flakes of snow falling.

She was alone in the camp in a drafty, unheated cabin. Certain that she was dying, the old woman bundled up and walked through the deserted camp in the light snow. In the evening she walked into the main street of a little suburban Long Island town and sat down on the corner.

When a Welfare Department worker found her, she was half covered with fresh snow. She had been looking for a place to die, and something about the corner reminded her of home.

Another crew leader, Horace Front, had a crew in North Carolina, but he had promised the grower a bigger one. While they were sitting out a rainy spell, Horace drove his bus back to Mississippi and got ten high school boys. None of them had any money, but Horace promised he'd take care of them. When he got back to camp in North Carolina, the crop still was not ready to pick. The boys went four days without eating. Conditions in the camp were getting dangerous, when the Welfare Department found out about it and offered to obtain surplus food for the crew. As crew leader, Horace would have to certify that the crew was without work. But Horace had other ideas. He wanted the Welfare Department to let him have the food so that he could give it to the crew. He insisted that it would hurt his reputation in Florida if it became known that his crew had "to take off welfare." It didn't seem to bother him that they were half starved.

What Horace wanted was to sell the food to the workers "on credit." When a case worker and a migrant minister checked on the camp, they found that Horace had decided to feed the crew himself rather than back down. He had made some pimento-cheese sandwiches and iced tea. Fortunately, the crop was ready the next day. Once they were working the crew would have money.

In another incident in North Carolina, a migrant driving a tractor was trapped under it when it turned over. The grower was furious that the tractor had been damaged. The crew leader had to fire the worker on the spot. During the argument over the tractor, the injured migrant was ignored.

The migrant minister who took him to the hospital said, "He was a big husky fellow. But he was hurt badly. While they argued about the tractor, he sat there between the rows holding his chest and crying like a baby."

A migrant worker in Belle Glade was burned by an insecticide. His whole face was a raw wound. The grower told him to see the crew leader because "that is his responsibility." The crew leader told him to get lost, which he did.

Usually a crew leader is able to protect the crew from mistreatment. "Freewheelers," who travel on their own, sometimes wish they had a crew leader to turn to. Two freewheelers stopped at a farm in South Carolina and got work. They had not eaten in two days. When they had made enough for a meal they started to a store across the road from the field. The grower saw them leaving and shouted, "Hey, nigger! Where you going?"

They said they were going for food. "No niggers walk off my farm without telling me!" He took a pistol out of his belt and fired at their feet. They ran.

The two men went to the Welfare Department and told them what had happened. A woman who worked there gave them a few dollars from her pocketbook. She suggested that since they were freewheelers, they'd better just keep on wheeling. It was all she could do.

There are many honest crew leaders like Juan Velez. Juan traveled with his family from Texas to the Dakotas, following sugar beets, fruits, and vegetables. He did pretty well by himself. When he got back to Texas, he found he had made $300 over his expenses. The next year his brother's family went along. After that, several families in the neighborhood started making the trip. Juan found himself with a crew of about thirty. To save on transportation, the crew bought an old bus.

Juan had verbal contracts with several farmers and they looked for him every year. Juan became more of a clan leader than a crew leader.

On the West Coast, the crew leader is called a labor contractor. (The term "crew leader" refers to the foreman.) Nick Peronni is a labor contractor in California. He has a fleet of buses and trucks that haul workers in and out of the San Joaquin Valley. He operates out of the "slave market," a big fenced-in lot that serves as a hiring hall. It is just up the street from the Farm Placement Service in the skid row section. Before a man can work, he has to get a white card from the placement office. If he changes crews, he can't get another card. Even if the grower cheats him, he'll lose his white card if he quits.

Most of the growers that Nick works for prefer to use contract workers from Mexico. Part of Nick's job is to keep too many of the local workers from getting on the crews. (The tactics used are described in Chapter Eight.)

Nick does not travel with the crews. He loads the buses out of the "slave market" each day for short day-hauls into the valley. He also handles the paper work and red tape of importing the Mexicans.

No one is sure how much Nick makes, but estimates run high. As he puts it, "If this thing blows up tomorrow, I'll go fishing. It'll be a long time before I get cold and hungry."

Juan Garcia is a labor contractor in Guadalajara, Mexico. He specializes in recruiting "braceros" (literally: "arm-men") in Mexico for growers in the Southwest. He makes his money by selling "letters of employment" to the Mexicans who want to go to the United States to work. He gets as much as $400 for a letter, plus the legal fees and bribes he has to pay.

These men represent the main kinds of crew leaders. No one knows how many are like Hamp and how many are like Juan Velez. For the most part their lives are hard to trace. Some use colorful pseudonyms like Sugar Daddy, Cool Breeze, or Meatball. Few of their crew members know their real names. A few years ago the *New York Times* reported that only half of the crew leaders coming into New York State gave addresses that could be located.

Tax investigators in Oregon found that "relatively few" crew leaders had ever filed personal income taxes, and "almost none" had filed Social Security returns for the crew, even though all presumably collected from their migrants.

The crew leader is an effective buffer between the migrant and the grower. Both like it that way, and despite the efforts of the Labor Department it looks as if that's the way it's going to remain.

Beginning in 1965, a crew leader will have to register with the Labor Department and obtain a certificate to do business. If he lies to his workers about wages, hours, or working conditions, deals in narcotics, gambling rackets, or prostitution, he can be fined a maximum of $500 and run the risk of losing his license.

Since there are now an estimated 12,000 crew leaders and labor contractors, the law may be difficult to police. And owing to the isolation and intimidation of the migrants, violations of the law will not always be reported. The law, nonetheless, is a good one—long in coming and certainly badly needed.

3

THE TAR-PAPER CURTAIN

The modern locus of poverty is even more the rural than the urban slum.

—JOHN KENNETH GALBRAITH, *The Affluent Society*

WHEN LITTLE JIM'S WEARY CREW arrived at the labor camp, the first thing they saw was the kerosene lantern. To migrant workers, this is a sign. And the sign is not good.

It tells them there is no electricity. And where this is lacking, there is usually no plumbing. An old camp with rickety shacks. On hot days the stench from the privies shrouds the camp. On rainy days the water does not drain and the cabins look like little swamp boats.

The crew always hopes for one of those new camps they have heard about—the ones with cement-block cabins and inside plumbing. Good migrant camps do exist, but if you follow the migrant stream for long, it becomes apparent that they are rare.

It is not possible for an urban nonmigrant American to imagine life in a migrant camp. But a quick illustration can give you a notion. In the middle of your living room, mark off a space eight feet wide and sixteen feet long. This represents half of a two-family cabin in a Princeton, Florida, camp where a thousand migrants live during the season. Here two families live in a cabin sixteen feet square.

If you put a few chairs in the space you have marked off, you begin to see how a room can close in. Try spending an evening in it. But imagine while you sit there that on the other side of a one-inch wall sits another family. When they walk around, your side of the cabin shakes.

Migrant camps are within commuting distance of Times Square, under the vapor trails of Cape Kennedy, and surrounded by missile sites in the Southwest. Some are behind barbed wire and even patrolled by armed guards.*

They have names like Tin Top, Tin Town, Black Cat Row, Cardboard City, Mexico City, The Bottoms, Osceola (for whites), and Okeechobee (for blacks).

Negroes from the Black Belt are dismayed by the camps they find up North. Okies and Arkies who migrate today find camps much like the Joads found in the *Grapes of Wrath* era. They may, in fact, find the same camps, but in worse shape.

You can drive from New York to California and never see a migrant camp. You have to know where to look. And you will not be welcome unless you are there to work. To borrow a popular analogy, a tar-paper curtain separates the migrant camps from the rest of America.

* In April of 1962, California Packing Corporation (Del Monte) placed armed guards around its Union Island Camp to keep out union organizers.

Let us look at a typical migrant camp, which we will call Shacktown. Shacktown is owned by a corporate farm. One of the foremen is in charge of the camp, "but mostly," he says, "we just turn it over to the people to run for themselves." In other words, no one collects garbage or maintains the camp in any way.

The camp is built on the grower's sprawling farm. You cannot reach it without trespassing, and several signs along the road remind the visitor of this. Even finding the camp is difficult. Local residents are suspicious of outsiders who are interested in migrant camps. Requests for directions are met with icy stares.

Shacktown was built about fifteen years ago. Although there are trees nearby, the camp is built on a barren red-clay hill, baked by a blazing summer sun. There are four barrack-type frame buildings, divided into single rooms. Few repairs have ever been made. Most of the screen doors are gone. The floors sag. The roofs leak. The Johnsons, a Shacktown family, have a six-month-old baby and five other children. "When it rains," said Mr. Johnson, "it leaks on our bed and all over the room. During the nights when it rains we have to stand up with the baby so he don't get wet and catch pneumonia."

All the rooms in Shacktown are the same size, eight by sixteen feet. When the Johnsons moved in, they found they needed much more space. They sawed through one wall, a single thickness of 1″ x 6″ pine, and made a door to the next room, which was not occupied.

The exterior walls are unpainted and uninsulated. They keep out neither wind nor rain, sight nor sound. Cracks between the boards are big enough to put your hand through. There is no privacy, and the Johnsons, like most Shacktown families, have learned to live without it.

The windows are simple cutouts, with a hatch propped up from the bottom. Some have a piece of clothlike screen wire tacked on.

The only touch of the twentieth century in the Johnsons' cabin is a drop cord that hangs down from the ceiling. It burns a single, overhead light bulb, plays a small worn radio, and on the rare occasions it works, an ancient television set Mr. Johnson bought for ten dollars. Through it, they get their only glimpse of urban, affluent America.

Behind the barracks are two privies, both four-seaters. The door to the women's privy is missing, but the rank growth of weeds serves as a door. There are no lights. No one uses the toilets after dark for fear of being hit over the head and robbed. The Johnsons use a "slop jar" at night. It is kept in the kitchen, and used for garbage, too.

There is virtually no hope of keeping out the flies that swarm around the privies. But one county health inspector found an unusual way of getting the growers interested in the problem. The inspector would drop by the grower's house just before lunch and ask to see the migrant camp. When they came to the privy, the inspector would throw a handful of flour over the seats, which invariably swarmed with flies. On the way back to the house, the inspector would manage to get invited for lunch.

At the table he would remark, "Well, I'm sure glad you asked us-all to lunch." And there, crawling around on the fried chicken, would be a floured, white-backed privy fly.

During most of the season in Shacktown there will be several full- or part-time whores. Prostitution thrives behind open doors. Venereal diseases are sometimes epidemic. (In a crew near Morehead City, North Carolina, one woman infected ten men in the course of three days. Out of eight crews working in the area, six had at least one syphilitic.)

There are two hasps on the Johnsons' door in Shacktown. One is for the family to use. The other is for the grower. If rent is not paid, the family will find, when they

return from the field, that they have been locked out.
(Some growers provide cabins free. Some charge accord-
ing to the number of able-bodied workers in the family.
Rents run as low as ten dollars a month to as high as fifty.)

The Johnsons, like most Shacktown families, do their
own cooking. But grocery shopping is not easy. There is
a small cracker-barrel store near the camp run by the
grower, but the prices are a third higher than in town.
"We got a ten-cent raise," said Mr. Johnson, "and everything in the store went up a quarter. He wants us to buy
from him or move out. It don't seem right."

If a man wants his money before payday, the grower
gives him an I O U (scrip) redeemable at his store.

Cooking is done on a small, unvented, open-flame kerosene stove, which serves as a heater in the cold weather.
Fires and explosions are not uncommon. The cabins are
not wired for electric heaters; gas is not available. Bottled
gas requires a deposit and an installation fee.

The cabins are unheated in spite of the fact that it gets
quite cold during the early harvest seasons. Asked if the
tenants didn't suffer from the cold nights, the camp manager replied, "Oh, heat's no problem. You'd be surprised
how hot it gets in one of them little cabins with so many
people."

For most of the year the cabins are miserably hot, There
is no ventilation through the single window opening. Re-
frigeration is nonexistent, and perishable foods seldom find
their way to the table. The baby's milk sours quickly, so he
is given warm Coke.

Good water is always scarce in Shacktown. Between
the long buildings there is a single cold-water tap. The
faucet leaks, and there is no drainage. A small pond has
developed, and the faucet is reached by a footbridge made
of boards propped on rocks. This is the only water in the
camp.

A hot bath for all of the Johnsons in a single evening is

a near impossibility. Just keeping clean is a struggle. Water must be carried in from the spigot, heated over the kerosene stove, and poured into the washtub. In the evening the eldest children are sent out with buckets to stand in line for water. Sometimes the Johnsons buy their water from a "water dealer" who sells it by the bucket. "We get some of our water down the road [about five miles]," said Mrs. Johnson. "Sometimes I get so tired I'd just like to go in and die.

"We have to boil the water and then take it to the tub to wash the clothes. We have to boil water for washing dishes. The last camp we was in had a shower, but you had to stand in line for it half a day, especially in the summer."

The problem of getting water is widespread in migrant camps. A Mexican national in California said his camp was without water for a week. "The contractor said the pump broke. There was a small rusty pipe that brought enough water for washing the hands and the face but we could not wash our clothes, and we could not take a bath for a week. He [the inspector] ordered that the pump be fixed right away. Now the water from the baths is pumped out of a big hole, and it flows through a ditch between the bunkhouse and the tents. When it makes warm weather it smells very bad. To me it looks like the contractor is not afraid of the inspector."*

When several children in a Swansboro, North Carolina, camp became ill, Rev. Jack Mansfield had the water in the camp tested. It was found to be contaminated. He reported this to the county health office. They said nothing could be done. The camp had been condemned long before.

One of the women in the camp said her grandchild almost died in Florida the previous season (1963). "Two thirds of the people in that camp had some kind of stomach trouble. That there baby would have died. He was skin and bones. Some said it was the water. Some said it was them chemical

* Ernesto Galarza, *Strangers in Our Fields.*

sprays. Doctors came into the camp, there was so many people sick."

The trouble could have been either sprays or the water. In 1959 a Dade County (Florida) grand jury "after investigating twelve cases of poisoning by parathion and other powerful new phosphorus organic compounds, found that if proper sanitation facilities had been provided, *six deaths could have been prevented by the 'simple expedient' of bathing in hot water* [italics added]."

A clean-up drive in Dade County led by Sanitarian C. P. Thayer resulted in vastly improved conditions. Still not things of beauty and comfort, the Dade migrant camps are the best in the nation.

Too often, local health officials lack either the will or the power to enforce the simplest sanitary regulations. A new law in Oklahoma gives the Health Department the power to close down a camp. "Of course," drawled one official, "it'd be real inter-restin to see what happened if they ever tried to close a camp."

Shacktown is a typical migrant camp, but not all migrants live like the Johnsons. Some find better camps. Many will find no room at all. These unfortunate workers will live "under the stars."

Three hundred migrants were stranded in Nevada when the harvest was late. The Associated Press reported on February 26, 1959: "For days they had barely enough food to keep alive. They camped—men, women and children—in the open, along ditch banks, without protection from winter rains and freezing night temperatures. They took their drinking water from irrigation ditches used by cattle. Many children were sick. And they had no work."

Thousands of workers were thrown out of work in 1960 and 1962 during the sudden freezes in Florida. They camped along the canals and irrigation ditches. They strung tar-paper tents between the trees and covered them with flattened tin cans. Bread lines were set up, and mass evictions began of many workers who could not pay the cabin rent in the camps.

In 1960 the cotton crop was lost in Arizona. In February the Migrant Ministry "counted six families living in cars or makeshift dwellings of cardboard and tin—no water and no sanitary facilities.

"Many of our migrant families have no other home than their old car. A family of 11 had been living in their car for three months, from December to March 1958. Included in the family was a three-month-old baby, and another two years of age, and the rest from four to fourteen. The older children were two years behind their age level in school.

"All suffered from malnutrition and were unbearably dirty. One family living in their car had been without food for several days. When we investigated we found five children and the parents asleep in the car, and two children crowded in the trunk with the lid down."

In Oregon a Labor Department report noted: "Bed rolls were spread on the ground, or tarpaulin and stick arrangements gave semishelter. One ingenious migrant who had recently married a very attractive and well-dressed woman . . . constructed a neat shack out of paper boxes."

In towns like Bakersfield, California, single migrant farm workers sleep in the jungles around the Kern River. The "aristocrats," according to City Manager Lee Gunn, camp in their jalopies along the highways "only to be moved along by law enforcement officers. Some try to make public parks a sleeping place.

"These lone, transient men . . . are dumped out of labor buses in the city at night . . . Some cities allow transient workers to spend some time in seats of bus stations, but they're soon moved on by the police. . . In the wintertime or in wet weather he cannot sit on park benches in our city parks . . . He can buy a schooner of beer and watch a fifteen-minute TV show in a bar but unless he keeps a drink in front of him, he will soon be unwelcome. So . . . he must go back to his room, if he has one, or find himself a makeshift place to sleep for the night."*

Migrant workers are often housed with the livestock. A Mexican worker in California described his camp this way: "We are installed in a barn which was used for the cows when we moved in. You have to slide the big door and go in and out the same as the cows. The cracks between the wall planks are about eight or ten centimeters wide. This makes very good ventilation for the cattle but it allows the wind to pass over our bunks at night . . . It is strong and fresh cow smell. It is necessary to use much Flit and the smell of this chemical also affronts us. The Americans are very inventive. Perhaps someday they will invent a Flit with perfume . . . The only person who comes to see us is the Father who hears confessions and says the Rosary. We are ashamed for him on account of the smell of the cows and the stink of the Flit."

Dr. Ernesto Galarza, who interviewed this worker, is a quiet, scholarly man, and a long-time observer of migrant America. He found Mexican workers in California in some strange camps: a storage shed, a chick hatchery, a small building with boarded-up windows, a dairy barn, a stable, tents in various stages of wear and tear, abandoned World War II barracks, and tumble-down Quonset huts.

When the old Farm Security Administration built the migrant labor camps in the Depression years, they built just about all the decent housing the migrants ever had. Now the FSA camps have either been torn down or turned over to the cities, where they are still open to migrants who can afford the rent. The FSA camps that are left usually have a manager who sees to it that the camp is clean and the rents are paid.

* *California's Farm Labor Problems*, Part I, 1961 (the Cobey Committee).

A few motel-type migrant camps have been built in recent years, but most are for foreign workers. Both the British and Mexican governments require certain minimal standards of housing.* The "motel" camp is similar in design to Shacktown, but it is made of cement blocks. The floors, tables, bedsteads, and kitchen counters are made of solid concrete. Some even have running hot and cold water in the rooms, an almost unheard-of luxury.

In California, Michigan, New Jersey, Oregon, and Florida improvements have been made in migrant housing. Yet, in the words of Edith Lowry, former director of the Migrant Ministry: "The picture today is not too different from what it was thirty years ago in terms of inhumanity and deprivation in the way in which families have to live."

If there is a rule-of-thumb in migrant housing, it is summed up in the telling phrase: "Reasonable protection against the weather." A farm management textbook in 1921 in a chapter on Tramp Laborers advised that "these men should be provided with a reasonably warm, dry place to sleep, but as a rule no special housing is needed for them."

Three decades later, in 1951, a state supervisor of the Farm Placement Service was asked if he had a standard of housing to be followed before sending workers to a farmer. He replied, "No, no, sir. In other words, it must be a question of at least reasonable protection against the weather. That is about as far as we can go."

In 1963 the same question was put to a placement service director in Benton Harbor, Michigan. His criterion was "a reasonable protection against the elements."

In Oklahoma City, Laymon Crump, the information director of the Placement Service, put it a little more bluntly. "Well, that's all they [the migrants] want. I mean, all they

---

* These standards are not always met, as we have seen. But new construction has been for offshore workers (from Puerto Rico and the West Indies) or braceros (Mexican farm workers). "The squeaky wheel," said Benjamin Franklin, "gets the oil."

want is just a partition so that this man don't sleep with that man's wife. And if you put in toilets, they'd use the hall."

The Labor Department's *Farm Labor Fact Book* describes the housing needs of migrants thusly: "Migrant farm workers travel long distances and may be away from their home bases for months at a time. One of their most urgent problems is finding places to stay . . . It is not necessary that these accommodations be elaborate. The migrants themselves are accustomed to hardships."

As bad as conditions are in the camps where the migrants live, they are worse in the fields where they work. A Florida Health Department report noted that at times crews refused to harvest fields because of the human waste deposited there by an earlier crew.

Americans are probably the most dirt-conscious people in the world. We are a bathroom-oriented society. Chains of restaurants, motels, and hotels across the country became successful not because the food was excellent or the rooms charming, but on the almost sole merit that the establishments were spotlessly clean.

In such a society it is not pleasant to imagine that beneath the cellophane wrapper lies a head of lettuce that has been urinated on. A storm of controversy erupted when a labor union showed a movie of field workers urinating on a row of lettuce. Growers charged that the picture was posed by union men in old clothes. Whether this was true or not is beside the point. If it was, it need not have been.

The fields of the modern factory farm are immense. And there are no bathrooms. A Catholic priest observed that "most consumers would gag on their salad if they saw these conditions, the lack of sanitary conditions, under which these products are grown and processed."

After a tour of leading farm states, Senator Harrison Williams of New Jersey said, "In the fields . . . sanitation facilities are a rarity. Unlike other sectors of our commerce, agriculture generally does not provide migrant farm workers with field sanitation facilities, such as toilets, hand-washing facilities, and potable drinking water.

"We as consumers have good reason to be uneasy about this situation. Much of our soft food and other products are picked, and often field-packed, by migratory farm workers. If we object to filth anywhere, we certainly should object to it in any part of the process that brings the food from the fields to our tables. Quite often the next hand to touch the celery after that operation in the fields will be ours when we buy it in the store to take it home.

"This is true of other fruits and vegetables—from the tree, from the ground, into a hamper, and into your house —picked by people who do not have any facilities for sanitation where they are working eight hours a day."

One grower, a woman who looked a little like Tugboat Annie, docked the workers an hour's pay if they left the field to go to the bathroom. The woman stayed with the crew most of the day. The men had to relieve themselves in front of her. They found this humiliating but were unwilling to lose the wage.

Antonio Velez, a field worker in the San Joaquin Valley, said he was told by the grower to take a pickup truck into the fields which carried two chemical toilets. The grower told him to drive fast so that the toilets would slosh around and be dirty. Then no one would want to use them. The grower was afraid the workers "would lose too much time going to the bathroom."

The idea of providing field workers with toilets and clean water strikes most growers as an outrageous refinement. Consumers who are aware that diseases such as amoebic dysentery, polio, and infectious hepatitis (to name only a few) can be transmitted through human excreta may not be so ready to belittle the importance of field sanitation.

Dysentery is often a subject for jokes. It is called by

a host of humorous euphemisms. The facts about dysentery are less funny. It kills 6,000 Americans a year, finding its heaviest toll among children less than two years old, many of whom are the children of migrant workers.

It will be argued that to supply field workers with rest rooms would be prohibitively expensive. In 1955, as a result of newspaper articles and state investigations about the lack of bathrooms and hand-washing facilities, a group of western lettuce growers started a voluntary program. A novel type of mobile toilet and hand-washing unit was developed and put to trial in the lettuce fields, and turned out to be successful.

Forty of the units were built and put into the fields in the spring of 1956. None of the other growers picked up the idea, so when pressure abated, the project was abandoned.

James Agee described a tenant family over two decades ago, in *Let Us Now Praise Famous Men*. It serves, unaltered, as a valid description of what passes for migrant "sanitation."

"These families lack not only 'plumbing' but the 'privies' which are by jest supposed to be the property of any American farmer, and the mail-order catalogues which, again with a loud tee-hee, are supposed to be this farmer's toilet paper. They retire to the bushes; and they clean themselves as well as they can with newspaper if they have any around the house, otherwise with corncobs, twigs, or leaves. To say they are forced in this respect to live 'like animals' is a little silly, for animals have the advantage on them on many counts. I will say, then, that whether or not The Bathroom Beautiful is to be preached to all nations, it is not to their advantage in a 'civilized' world to have to use themselves as the simplest savages do."

Most growers will readily admit the need for field sanitation, although few do anything about it.

Some growers, however, have yet to even admit that a

problem exists with migrant camps. The executive secretary of the powerful Vegetable Growers Association of America (VEGA) complained that "it has even been said that farmers provide better housing for pigs than they do for their workers. We resent these half-truths, misleading statements, and distorted views that have been perpetrated upon the American public regarding migrant housing. In the great majority of the cases the picture that has been painted simply is not true." But then he remarked that "large investments in land, machinery, and operating capital *leave very little for housing facilities* [italics added]."

A bill was recently in committee that would give domestic American workers the same guarantees of decent housing that foreign workers have long held. *VEGA* magazine called the bill "infamous" and commented, "We hope to *keep it bottled up,* because if it does come out of committee, *we've had it* [italics theirs]." The bill never came out.

Seasonal farm workers who live and work in a single farming area often live only a little better than the migrants. The Robertson family lives in one of the many small towns that dot the San Joaquin Valley. For nine months of the year they work in the fields and groves that are near their home. But for the late summer and early fall they go up to Oregon for cherries and apples. The Robertsons consider themselves seasonal farm workers. In spite of the fact that they go to Oregon every year, they would be insulted if you called them migrants.

The community they live in is made up of just such people. Most of them have managed to put down a small down-payment on a house. In California particularly, there are many communities made up of people who are residents most of the year but who do migrate. The Robertsons came to California as migrants during the early forties.

They have managed to escape from the stream almost entirely. Their trip to Oregon is made when the children are out of school, and the whole family really looks forward to it, since they are well received in Oregon.

But all across the country, wherever the migrant stream runs, rural slums rise, made up entirely of little huts tacked together from boxes, fences, car bodies, buses, and billboards, tied together with wire and propped together with poles. "You can drive through these woods," said a resident of Riverhead, Long Island, "and not see anyone for miles. Next week you come by, and there'll be a little shack nailed to a tree and a family living in it."

Migrants become desperate for land. So strong is their desire for a home that they will practically buy anything offered to them if they can afford the down-payment. A thriving business is done by rural slumlords who subdivide almost worthless land and sell it to migrant escapees. When the migrant hits "corn bread" living, and misses payments, the slumlord reclaims the property and resells it. Promised sewer connections, water lines, and new roads are seldom, if ever, delivered.

These rural slums are "shoestring communities," and the people in them cease to be migrants but acquire a new status, hardly more flattering—"shoestringers."

The large rural-urban centers are jumping-off places for prospective shoestringers. In California, New Jersey, Michigan, Florida, New York, Illinois, and Ohio, the migrant flees the stream.

In Rochester, New York, Negroes who witnessed and participated in the riots that tore up that city in July of 1964 said the agricultural migrants were a contributing cause to the trouble. The Negro section, as effectively Jim Crow as any in the South, is overcrowded with the resident population. When the seasonal workers arrive, they settle not only in the migrant camps but in the marginal

housing in the Negro slum. The southern migrants, illiterate, poor, desperate for work and housing, crowd and
upset the already tense community.

One of the most famous shoestring communities is Three
Rocks, California. It is a town made up entirely of farm
workers, many of them "part-time" migrants like the
Robertsons. Three Rocks was recently featured in a Mos-
cow daily paper as an example of life down on the American farm. It was impossible to exaggerate. A subsequent
investigation revealed that the town was virtually without
bathrooms, water, and sewage systems, and all the housing
was dilapidated and deteriorated.

There are rural slums like this all over America. They
are part of what we call our "invisible" poverty.

4

THE CHILDREN OF
HARVEST

INQUEST: . . . The body is that of a well-developed, moderately emaciated white male infant—approximately four months old . . .

FATHER'S TESTIMONY: "On November fourth, he started vomiting, but stopped and seemed better. About nine o'clock on Sunday, the sixth, he was very bad, and we started for the hospital. We took him to the Coalinga Hospital but we didn't have any money and they sent us to the General Hospital in Fresno. We are not familiar with this area and we stopped at the Wallace Sanatorium. We didn't have any money so they sent us to the General Hospital. When we arrived they told us the baby was dead."

*—Report of the President's
Commission on Migratory Labor*

THE MAN put down his hamper. "It sure looks like rain," he said. The skies were a bright crystal-blue, with only a trace of clouds to the east. The crew kept working, but a few looked up and saw the three men coming down the row.

One was the grower, who seldom came around. The other was the crew leader. The third man was a stranger. He carried a brown leather case and a clip-board. The men just nodded as they passed.

They went up and down the rows, the first two walking easily. The third man, the stranger, stumbled now and then—a city man used to flat sidewalks.

They crossed the red-clay road and went into the south field. A woman looked up as they came past the stacks of empty crates. Before they were close enough to hear, she turned to the busy crew. "Sure looks like rain."

Two small pickers dropped their boxes, darted through the vines, and ran into the woods. Someone on the next row passed the word. "Sure looks like rain." Two more children ducked into the vines and ran.

The children hid beyond the road in a small clearing in a clump of scrub oaks. From here they could see the man leave. It was their favorite game. Hiding from the inspector was about the only thing that broke up the long hours in the field. In the camp they played hide-and-seek this way. When you were "it" you were the inspector. But it was more fun when there was a real inspector, like now.

Luis was the eldest of the children. He had been to school off and on, but by the time he was twelve, he had only started the fourth grade. If he ever went back he would be in the fifth grade because he was older and bigger now.

But Luis didn't want to go back. He wanted to run away. He had been around the country a lot. The year before, they went to California and Oregon. One year they went to Arkansas. Once, long ago—he was too young to remember—his father took them to Florida for the winter citrus harvest.

Luis seemed to be an ageless child. He had a way of taking a deep, weary drag on a cigarette and after a long while letting the smoke curve slowly out of his nostrils. His face was wrinkled, marked with a tiny network of fragile lines at the corners of his eyes and deeper lines across his forehead.

Still, being a child, he liked to play games. And enjoyed the gaiety at the Christmas feast. But at the end of the working day, he would stand slightly stooped, with his hands stuck flat into his back pockets. From behind he looked like a dwarf—a tiny old man whose bones had dried up and warped with age.

Billy was the youngest of the children. He was not quite five, but old enough to do a little work. He didn't earn much, but it was better, his father said, than having him sit around the day-care center, which cost them seventy-five cents every single day.

His mother kept the money he earned in a Mason jar. When fall came, he'd get a pair of shoes if there was enough money. He could start school, if there was one nearby, in new shoes.

His brother lay beside him in the clearing. John was ten. In the years that separated Billy and John, a brother and sister had died, unnamed, a day after birth. John kept them alive in his imagination. There were few playmates in the camps and fields that he ever got to know.

"I got two brothers and a sister," he would say. "And they's all in heaven but Billy there."

He called his invisible brother Fred, which is what he wanted to be called instead of John. Faith was the name he gave his sister. He saw her as soft and gentle, wearing a dress with white frills, like a china doll.

He played over in his mind a single drama with endless

variations. Faith was hurt or being picked on by some bully. He would come to her side to help or defend her. Then he and Faith and Fred would sit beneath a tree, and they would praise him for his bravery, and he would say it was nothing. They would have something cold to drink and maybe some candy to eat.

He retreated more and more into this pleasant world. His mother had noticed his blank gaze many times and had heard him say "Faith." She thought he was going to be called to the ministry to be a gospel preacher or a faith healer.

Robert was almost as old as Luis. He had been on the season for two years. His father came from the sawmill one day and said, "They don't need me any more. They hired a machine." His father had tried to make a joke of it, but late at night Robert could hear his mother crying. He knew it wasn't a joke about the machine being hired.

They sold their house and packed everything into the car. Robert left school, and now they lived in one camp after another. Sometimes they slept in the car.

The man with the clip-board left. The children came out of the bushes, picked up their boxes. They bent over in silence and began to pluck at the vines.

These are the children of harvest. "The kids that don't count" they are sometimes called. "The here-today-gone-tomorrow kids."

Inspectors from the Department of Labor find children working illegally on 60 percent of the farms they inspect. And no one knows how many hide in the woods when "it looks like rain."

No one really knows how many migrant children there are. Estimates run from 100,000 to 600,000. The most frequently used figure is 150,000.

In some areas much of the harvest work is done by children. One survey in the olive groves of California showed that nearly three fourths of the workers were children.

An Oregon survey showed the importance of the child's labor to the family. There the average migrant worker earned $32 a week during the weeks he worked. But his wife and children earned together $48. (In some crops women and children do more than half the harvest work.)

The average American child is the most overfed and overprotected in the world. His parents are eager that his education be the best they can afford. The happiness of the child is their constant goal.

The entire entertainment industry is his court jester. The toy maker who captures the child's fancy is amply rewarded. The child is constantly being appraised by sociologists and psychologists. Like one amorphous parent, the nation frets and broods, exclaims and applauds.

As a young adult he ventures out into the world with every chance of success. For the migrant child, almost the reverse is true. He gets none of the attention so lavished upon his nonmigrant contemporaries.

His chance of breaking out of the migrant cycle into normal society is slim. He is a child of the soil and knows not of the world of the city. It is a well-worn saying that today you need a college education just to get in line for a job. The migrant child has, on the average, a fourth-grade education. Even with this, he may be illiterate. A migrant minister in Florida took a young man he had known for years down to the courthouse to help him obtain a marriage license. The man had worked as a migrant and had got to the tenth grade before he quit school. When he started to sign the license, he had to admit to the minister that he couldn't write. He had never learned, because the family moved around with the crops. He was ashamed of it and was very withdrawn in class.

Wherever he went to school, it was always for a few months here or a few weeks there. His teachers had no time for this shy little boy who was going to leave school anyway. He was promoted from grade to grade on the "social advancement" principle—no child may be held in the same grade more than two years. As a result, according to a social worker in New York State, illiterate students have been graduated from high schools.

Many states have carried on experimental programs for educating migrant children, but their total effect has been slight. Colorado started a special summer school program that reached 300 of the 3000 migrant children in the state.

The birth of the migrant child will most likely be in a migrant shack or, at best, in the emergency room of a county hospital. His nursery is the field, and his toys the things that grow there. A few camps have day-care centers. There are only 24 registered centers in the United States. They have a total capacity of less than a thousand children.

The migrant child may never develop any idea of home. His family is never in any place long enough, and home to him is wherever he happens to be.

He seldom sees a doctor. It is almost certain that he will have pin worms and diarrhea. These diseases are so common that migrant parents think this is just the way children are.

Other untreated common ailments are: contagious skin infections, acute febrile tonsillitis, lymphadenopathy, asthma, iron-deficiency anemia, and disabling physical handicaps.

A doctor visiting a labor camp discovered in one family the fruits of neglect. Their five-year-old daughter had not been to a doctor in three years. She was totally deaf and had learned to speak only three words. She was about to start going to the camp school.

Her six-year-old brother had a wringer injury of his arm that had developed serious complications. The one-year-old baby had had diarrhea for over two weeks. The mother had to carry it two miles to the hospital. The father had stomach ulcers, which were not being treated.

A poor diet condemns the child from the start. A report on a camp in Mathis, Texas, showed that 96 percent of the children had not drunk milk in six months. Their diet consisted mainly of corn meal and rice. A doctor commenting on the report said there was evidence of "ordinary starvation."

The migrant child is prone to scurvy, rickets, kwashior-kor—a severe protein deficiency. Some reports have put the incidence of dental abnormalities at 95 percent, and others said that bad teeth were "universal."

Epidemics, like the one in the San Joaquin Valley a few years ago, take a heavy toll. Shigellosis, a form of dysentery, had been rampant in the valley for years. The infant mortality rate was extremely high. Within a short time, twenty-eight babies died of "dehydration and malnutrition." Contributing factors to the epidemic were primitive outhouses and crowded one-room cabins where as many as five children slept in a single bed.

The migrant child is also prey to a host of diseases now rare in the nonmigrant world: smallpox, diphtheria, and whooping cough. A medical survey in California showed that two thirds of the children under three years of age were never immunized against diphtheria, whooping cough, lockjaw, or smallpox. And two thirds of the children under eighteen had not received poliomyelitis immunization. Once a contagious disease has been discovered, it is difficult to check its spread. (There was a case of diphtheria in a migrant camp in western North Carolina last year. Health officials tried to track down all the people who were exposed to the sick child. Some were two states away before they were found.)

There have been many brave attempts to provide migrant workers with medical service. They are usually done on a shoestring budget and the energy of a few determined people in a community.

A migrant health bill was passed in 1963—and expires

in 1965. Under this bill, the Federal Government made grants available to nonprofit organizations and to individuals seeking to establish health programs for migrants. In most cases, this resulted in important increases in medical service. But often it provided nominal salaries for volunteers who previously were uncompensated.

The nature of migrancy makes adequate medical service difficult enough, but the residency requirements of most states exclude migrants from local welfare programs. The quiet tragedies, like the one quoted from the President's Commission at the beginning of this chapter, continue. During the summer of 1964, a little girl in a migrant camp near Cedarsville, New Jersey, swallowed some gasoline. The hospital refused to take her. She died the next day.

In the little farming towns around Morehead City, North Carolina, Jack Mansfield, a young minister, got together the first mobile medical clinic—a white trailer called the Rocking Horse, equipped with the rudiments of a doctor's office. The Rocking Horse—so named because it tilted back and forth when you walked around in it—was staffed by a group of local doctors who took turns going out to the migrant camps. The Welfare Department was persuaded to provide a social worker. The National Council of Churches provided a migrant minister.

By the light of a flickering kerosene lantern, the lines of workers waited to see the doctor. Some had unnamed miseries of the head, miseries of the chest; illusive aches and pains that moved up the back and seized the neck in a vise. Colds, bad teeth, rheumatism, and chronic headaches could only be treated with the same white pills.

On a night in late July, the Rocking Horse made its last visit to the camps. The lantern was hung high on a pole, and a small gasoline motor generated enough electricity to light the inside of the trailer and run a movie projector that showed a film on health and a cartoon.

Word was sent to the nearby camps that the doctor had come. It was a still, dark night. The lights from the trailer and the hammering sound of the little motor were enough to inform the nearest camps.

They came out of the darkness, tired and still covered with the fine dust from the field. They looked like a civilian army, straggling in after a lost battle. Some hung back in groups of two and three. Others began to form a line at the doorway of the trailer and give the social worker their names. For hours men, women, and children appeared from the darkness beyond the circle of light cast by the lantern. The last was a boy of fourteen.

He was heavy-set, with a constant, nervous smile. He had cropped tobacco all summer. But when he bent over, he said, he got dizzy and there was a ringing in his ears. The doctor listened to his heart, and wrote out a prescription for some medicine to hold down his high blood pressure. The doctor's advice was ironic. "Don't bend over," he said, "and don't overexert yourself. See a doctor regularly."

The boy held on to his smile as if he were waiting for the doctor to tell him he would be all right. After the boy had left the doctor closed up the little office. "I don't know what to tell him. If he doesn't do what I told him, he'll be dead before he's twenty. But does he understand? When can he see a doctor again?"

The lights flickered, and the motor was quieted. They stood in the sudden silence. Reverend Mansfield stopped at the door of his car. "Sometimes it seems we are on a train platform. These people come traveling by, and we try desperately to help them. They go on, and often we never see them again. And we seldom know if we've helped any.

"Last year we found a baby in one of the camps with worms so bad they were crawling out of its mouth. We took it to Duke Hospital in Durham. At first they didn't want to take it because it was a charity case. We managed to get the baby in by the back stairs, and then they *had* to take it. The doctors said the baby had the worst case of worms they had ever seen. He would have died in another day. The family was back in camp this year. And the baby is fine and healthy. When the mother saw us, she said, 'Yawl's next to Jesus.' "

A migrant child spends his life in an impoverished, primitive world, a stranger to life beyond the fields. He grows up without a childhood, to face the almost certain prospects of a life of grinding poverty.

It would take a full staff of psychologists to evaluate the psychic condition of the migrant children. Very little, if any, of this kind of attention has been given to them.

But even in the absence of any thorough-going study, the symptoms of frustration, bitterness, and disorganization are easy to see.

A day-care center for migrant children was set up in the basement of an Arkansas church. One of the most successful parts of the center was a workshop run by a young man named Alec Johnson. The shop was in a corner room, with small windows for ventilation at the top. It was always cool and pleasant on the hottest days.

Alec had assembled the usual carpentry tools and some leather-working tools. By the end of the season, when the migrants pulled out, he had learned several things about migrant children by watching them at play. One child who had character traits typical of some migrant children was Joey Smith. Joey was a blond, blue-eyed boy from Kentucky. The family had been on the road for almost ten years, which was most of Joey's life. He was two when the coal mine closed and his father lost his job.

When Joey first came to the shop he was quiet, at least for the first week. By the end of the second week he was racing around the room banging the chairs with a hammer.

Alec had to take it away from him, and Joey sulked and refused to do anything.

Alec got Joey interested in making a leather billfold. "I got all the material together," said Alec, "and Joey started with a flurry of energy. But within an hour he had put it aside and was toying with some pieces of lumber. I started him back on the billfold. Joey gave it a few whacks with the mallet and then looked around for something else to do. Joey wanted the billfold and had been excited about making it. But he didn't seem to be able to stay with it and finish.

"There were many of the kids who were like this. It seemed to be a characteristic. They start out with great enthusiasm, but as soon as they hit a snag, they toss whatever it is aside and go to something else. They haven't had any experience in building anything or in solving problems. They have no confidence in themselves."

There had been a news item in the local paper about the Aswan High Dam. Joey's family had evidently talked about it. The United States was at that time going "to help build it." Joey had gotten the idea that "they" were going to send him and his family over to Egypt to work on the dam.

"He talked about this quite a bit one morning. He was sure 'they' were going to make his family build the dam. Most of this came from the feeling many migrants have about the government. They think Uncle Sam is a great friend of all foreigners. Mexicans have been allowed to come in and take jobs away from them. Every day they see where another million dollars has gone to foreign aid. And here they are without a place to sleep. Their main contact with the government is through the Farm Placement Service. Most of the placement people are more interested in recruiting for the growers than in helping the migrants. It seems like the growers and the government are together. Most of the people who come here think this day-care center is run by the government. This puts us with the growers and the Farm Placement Service. The kids hear this from their parents.

"When I asked Joey who he thought was going to send him to Egypt, he said, 'They is. All them people.'

" 'But who are *they?*' I asked him. He looked at me, wide-eyed. 'You,' he said and ran out the door. He hasn't been back."

Books written on teaching migrant children stress that the teacher "see the child as an individual" and speak in terms "meaningful to the child."* A few sample texts have been tailored with this in mind. In a peculiar way of their own, they give an accurate picture of migrant life. A fourth-grade arithmetic text reads:

> Your father earns $20 a week. Your mother earns $15 a week. Your brother earns $18 a week. How much does your family earn together?

An interesting combination of "terms meaningful to the child" and a lack of understanding of the child is found in a song, "Calling for Migrants." The term "migrant" is strongly objected to by most of the harvesters. And yet this song is taught in the day-care centers:

> And when the crop is ready to pick,
> The farmer calls, "Come, migrants, quick!"
> "There's stooping to do, and reaching too,
> And that is why I call for you!"
> *Refrain:*
> Calling for migrants
> Calling for migrants
> There's stooping to do, and reaching too

* Louisa Shotwell, a writer for the National Council of Churches, told of a teacher who said "carry one" in a math class. None of the children understood. Finally one little boy asked, "Do you mean 'tote one'?"

And that is why I call for you.
(Repeat refrain to *tra-la-la*)

Teachers, doctors, and ministers have the most contact with the migrant children. They are, understandably, not optimistic about the future. A doctor from Texas painted this gloomy picture:

"The children of migrant parents are born into a world completely of their own. An anemic mother, and possibly a tubercular father—a life that will take him into his world where he may possibly die within one year, either from diarrhea, tuberculosis, or malnutrition. His infancy would be a very close association with his brothers and sisters. Their home would be a one- or two-room shack with no inside running water and no flush toilets. If he lives to be of school age, he could possibly go to many schools on different occasions at different places, but will never average more than three years of schooling in his lifetime. His future life will be one of wandering, poverty, and more sickness.

"As a migrant, his world will be from the Atlantic to the Pacific—from the Great Lakes to the Rio Grande. It will be his world, however, only in that the only piece of property he will own will be his grave.

"I may be here because I am still haunted by that remembrance of a day ten years ago when the little boy came to my office to ask me to go and see his mother who was sick. I went to his home—a one-room shack. I found a dead mother with six children lying in the same bed, all covered with blood from the hemorrhage of a dying tubercular mother."

As a footnote to this, a psychologist in Suffolk County, Long Island, has predicted an increase in criminal behavior among Negro migrants. He bases his prediction on the high incident of psychosis among migrant children. "This is caused by many things," he said, "among them a feeling of frustration, loss of hope, and withdrawal as the child becomes aware of his place in the world."

Few people can view this world of migrant children without coming away with a heavy heart. No one likes to see children mistreated. Lady Bird Johnson spoke for the whole country when she said that children were entitled to their childhood. One can only conclude that the good and reasonable people of America are not aware of what goes on in the fields of big agriculture.

Children have been working on the farm since the first farmer had a son, and it has always been considered part of the rural way of life. But there is a difference between the farmer's boy doing his chores and the migrant child topping onions and digging potatoes. The two are blurred together in the minds of most people outside of agriculture. The blurring gets help from such spokesman as North Carolina's Congressman Cooley who enunciated the Blue Sky Doctrine. "There are no sweatshops on the farms of America," he said. "On the farms of our nation, children labor with their parents out under the blue skies."

Under the blue skies of Idaho, a twelve-year-old girl got her pony-tail caught in a potato-digging machine. It ripped off her scalp, ears, eyelids, and cheeks. She died shortly afterward in a hospital.

On a farm in California, a ten-year-old girl came back from the fields exhausted from a day's work. She fell asleep on a pile of burlap bags as she waited for her parents. As other workers returned from the fields, they tossed the empty bags on the stack, and the little girl was soon covered up. A two-ton truck backed across the pile and drove off. They did not find her body until the next day.

If children were mangled in steel mills, there would be a storm of public protest. But death and injury on the mechanized farms seem to pass unnoticed. Under the blue sky of the farm factory is no place for little children. Agriculture is one of the three most hazardous industries. In

California alone, over 500 workers under the age of eighteen are seriously injured every year.

There is, of course, plenty of safe but hard work on the big farms for boys in their teens. During the summer months or even after school, they could work in the harvest.

A few of the big growers like Stokely-Van Camp have employed college students for field work in the summer. But according to Jon Misner, who is in charge of migrant labor, "By the time all the taxes are taken out, it doesn't leave them much. Most of them give it up."

Three students from Haverford tried their hand at the harvest in the West. A farmer hired them one day to chop beets (i.e., to weed the beets). "We worked ten hours one day, and the three of us earned less than five dollars together. We were being paid by the acre. None of us were fast enough. And we killed more beets than weeds."

The migrants who follow the harvest are the only people in America who are desperate enough for work to take it. The children they take with them will be another generation of wanderers, lost to themselves and to the nation.

PART TWO

Agribusiness

American Gothic by Grant Wood.
Courtesy of the Chicago Institute
of Art

5

FAREWELL TO GOTHIC AMERICA

If Democracy is to avoid the destiny of a faith that fades into mythology, its interpretation must have reality. It must either evolve with the times or be lost like the gods of Olympus. If at a time when farm families are so rapidly leaving the soil and 92 per cent of the population lives elsewhere, we continue to regard the family farm as a pillar of democracy, we may wake up to find the roof has caved in.

—EDWARD HIGBEE, *Farms and Farmers in an Urban Age*

IN SPITE of all that has happened to the American farm in the last few decades, we still think of the farmer in terms of Grant Wood's painting *American Gothic.* The farmer and his wife are of proud and simple bearing. She wears a calico dress and he a pair of faded overalls.

The farm of the Gothic Americans is a little place of forty acres, some pigs, a couple of cows, and a few chickens. With hard work and thrift, the family lives a God-fearing life, free of the tomfoolery and deceitful ways of the big city. This kind of family farm was the citadel of virtue in the classic rural tradition. Life was made hard by the vagaries of the weather, and complicated only by the bureaucrats in Washington.

While the family farm once held a central position in our national life and in forming our ideals and values, it no longer does. In 1900, when the population of the United States was under 76 million, 40 percent lived on the farm. Today, about 8 percent of the population live on the farm, and the percentage declines every year. The modern family farm bears little resemblance to the old-time farm, which is found only in the hearts and minds of that 92 percent of the people who live elsewhere.

Today the important farms, as units of production, are more like factories than rural citadels of virtue. Great cultivators and harvesting machines lumber through endless fields. Gangs of workers bring in the harvest. One cannot ride past these giant farms after the harvest is over and the crew departed, without an eerie feeling of being in a land without people. A verse from Isaiah rides the wind: "Woe to those who join house to house, who add field to field, until there is no more room, and you are made to dwell alone in the midst of the land."

The importance of making the distinction between the big farm and the little farm—between the factory-in-the-field and the American Gothic homestead—is essential to the story of migrant labor. To begin with, the family farmer and the migrant worker are in the same sinking boat. The family farm, while providing an income and a place to live, no longer contributes significantly to America's food production. If the earth suddenly swallowed up a million and a half small family farms in America—nearly half the total number—food production would drop by only 5 percent.

The big commercial farms produce most of our food. Half of it is produced by only 9 percent of the farms. These highly mechanized, capitalized, and integrated companies use most of the seasonal labor. Only a relatively few big growers (5 percent of the total number) use more than $2,000 worth of labor a year. The real giants—the top 3 percent—hire over one third of all farm labor.

It is through the field of the agribusiness farm-factories that the migrant stream flows. And these are the growers that bring foreign farm workers to America each year.

The growth of agribusiness, and its effect on the traditional family farm, has been watched with concern for many years. In 1923 the North Carolina Land Commission issued a still-urgent report:

> It is quite conceivable that under capitalistic or corporation farming, greater gains might be secured than under a system of small individual holdings.
>
> It is quite inconceivable, however, that the . . . farmer would be as good or as efficient a citizen, that he would take as great pride in farming, that he would get as much contentment and happiness for himself and his family out of his home, or that he could develop as satisfactory a community for himself and neighbors as he could and would if he owned the house in which he lives and the farm he cultivates. The problem, then, is that of life on the farm, the development of rural communities and the building of rural civilization with which, after all, we are most concerned . . . The late Governor Bicket said: "The small farm owned by the man who tills it is the best plant-bed in the world in which to grow a patriot . . . Every consideration of progress and safety urges us to employ all wise and just measures to get our lands into the

hands of many, and forestall that most destructive of all monopolies—the monopoly of the soil."

The policy of the federal government has always more or less agreed with this. Nearly every administration has declared itself in favor of preserving the family farm. It is ironic that each, in turn, has brought it closer to extinction.

In 1963 the government spent $4.7 billion on surplus commodities. Most of the money went to prosperous commercial farms, while only pennies trickled down to the hard-pressed family farms.

The government support price is often more than the production costs of the big commercial farms. This means they can produce without worrying about the market, since Uncle Sucker—as some of the farmers say—will buy what they cannot sell elsewhere.

In 1961 two corporate cotton farms received government subsidies of $2,000,000 each; thirteen great farms received $649,753 on the average; and 322 farms got $113,657 each. By contrast, 70 percent of the cotton farms got an average of $60. (The only government help to farm workers was the migrant health bill, passed in 1963.)

The government has subsidized the big operators in a more important way. The commercial farms have been allowed to draw on the pools of cheap labor from other countries, principally Mexico. The presence of hundreds of thousands of foreign workers has naturally disrupted the domestic labor market, resulting in low wages and poor working conditions. The family farmer, who hires little outside help, is forced to value his and his family's labor at no more than what the commercial farm pays for gang labor.

The exodus from the farm is proceeding at the rate of about 600,000–800,000 people a year.

The cities and towns have as little need at the present time for the surplus rural population as the nation does for the surplus farm production. It seems that the government would do better in spending our money by subsidizing small farmers instead of big-farm production.

It has been seriously suggested many times that over-production is caused by a surplus of farmers, and that we should let the natural laws of competition weed out the less successful. This way, the problem of surplus production and surplus farmers would solve itself at no expense to the taxpayers. But as we have already seen, most of the food is produced by relatively few big farms. The small farmers, who are frequently forced off the land by the competition, do not contribute significantly to the national output of food. And of course, when the small farmer finally gives up and goes to the city, he doesn't take his land with him. It is taken over eventually by another farmer and remains in production.

As a unit, the larger family farm is not without merit. According to a 1962 government report, "family farms [in this case those using 1.5 man-years of hired labor] are more efficient than large corporation-type farms . . . When the management of a farm is taken away from those who supply the labor, there is a loss of incentive, diligence, skill, and prudent judgment, which is necessary to maintain efficiency." The report said that the advantages of the corporate farm lay primarily in superior financing and control of the market.

Of course no farmer, whether big or small, can dominate the market. But the "vertically integrated" farm is its own market (*see* Chapter Eight). The perishable harvest from the field goes to the farm's own processing, canning, or freezing plants, and is sold under less urgent conditions than fresh produce. The small farmer selling perishable produce is completely at the mercy of the market, or more specifically, the buyer.

The position of the buyer is stronger today than it has ever been. In 1958 supermarket-buying agencies handled

60 percent of the food dollar. It is said that at the present time chain buyers account for 90 percent of the food dollar.

There are about 3.7 million farms in the United States. What seems to be happening is this: the 312,000 First Class farms are big and getting bigger. The 1,755,000 Middle Class farms are struggling. To survive, they need a more equitable marketing structure, some government aid, and a regulated farm labor force.

The Third Class farms, of which there are 1,641,000, are marked for certain death if agriculture continues for much longer on its present path. With them and their Middle Class brothers fades Gothic America.

6

IT ALL STARTED
WITH COLUMBUS

> . . . a bold peasantry, their country's pride,
> When once destroyed, can never be supplied.

—OLIVER GOLDSMITH, *The Deserted Village*

THE DROVES OF MIGRANT WORKERS that roam the country-side today are not new, nor are they there by accident. They fill a need as old as America.

The farm of the classic rural tradition—the family farm—required little outside labor. A hired man or two was enough on the bigger farm for most of the year. And at planting or harvest, neighboring farm families joined together and did the work, going from farm to farm.

The history of migrant labor is sketchy, but its dominant themes are quite clear. The rise of the corporate farm and the growth of the migrant labor force were twin developments. It is still argued which came first. Some say the industrialized farm developed because growers saw a chance to utilize a growing pool of unemployed labor. Others say that the development of the giant farm created a demand for gangs of itinerant labor, and the migrants came to fill the need. Whichever way it happened, the result was that the corporate farm is, and always has been, dependent on cheap migrant labor.

The distribution of land in the New World colonies set the stage for the development of our present agriculture. The factory farms developed first in the West and the Deep South, where land was distributed rather indiscriminately and in large chunks. As the commercial farm grew, it soon experienced difficulty in filling its brief demands for large numbers of workers. America was settled without a peasant class, so one had to be created and held in place either by force, intimidation, or poverty.

The first real seasonal farm workers were captured and enslaved Indians. "It was Christopher Columbus who first instituted the encomienda [assignments of Indians to work the soil] in America when he decreed that subdued tribes should assign Indians in sufficient number to develop and maintain the haciendas [land grants] of his conquistadors."*

The conquistadors were conquerors, not farmers and settlers. They had plenty of land, and wanted the Indians to work it for them. But they were never able to hold down enough Indians to make it profitable.

Much later, the southern plantation owner was more successful. By using African slaves he was able to combine, for the first time, large grants of land with a large, though captive, supply of labor.

* Edward Higbee, *Farms and Farmers in an Urban Age.*

The migrant force of today still bears the marks of history. Since early America was largely rural, farm interest dominated the government. While the problems created by the industrial revolution were often solved by law and a growing labor movement, agriculture has escaped most of the social legislation passed since the turn of the century. Agriculture has grown from a society, or a way of life, into a complex food industry, without settling up with its labor force. Had the Ford Motor Company been able to import cheap labor from underdeveloped countries, it is unlikely that automotive unions would have made much headway.

The commercial farm has never adjusted to the realities of modern labor conditions or wages. Furthermore, the modern commercial farmer holds on to the idea that somehow he has a God-given right to unlimited cheap labor.

Never has he had to enter the labor market and make serious efforts to attract farm labor. If anything characterizes the history of the seasonal farm worker, it is this: fate, through famine or depression, war or revolution, has time and again delivered to the commercial grower an ample supply of cheap and docile labor.

Most of the early colonizers (four out of five) were farmers. In New England and the middle colonies and in nearly all the frontier settlements, townspeople and families worked together at planting and harvesting. In Massachusetts, farmers could draft workers. The government set wages for sowing and reaping. The artisan or mechanic who had no farm of his own was likely to find himself called to the harvest by the local constable. There was also some slave traffic in Indian women and children who were captured in war. This practice, surprisingly enough, continued until the beginning of the eighteenth century.

But the problem of harvest labor was never acute in New

England. Each settler made a small claim and lived on it. Land speculation was unknown. Each man took only the land he needed.

Aside from the Africans, the largest part of the early work force (almost all agricultural) were voluntarily and involuntarily indentured servants. They were a varied lot of criminals, debtors, vagrants, exiles, and stunned men shanghaied from the streets of London.

The bigger farms were in the middle colonies and the South. Here land was distributed by "headright." A headright was a fifty-acre grant given to every new settler. But businessmen and sailors traveling back and forth between England and the New World picked up a headright on every crossing. Names were taken off old tombstones and record books and used for headright applications. And there was no restriction on what land could be claimed. A settler could get a whole valley by taking his fifty acres out of the middle.

The king made large grants of land to his friends in hopes of re-establishing feudalism, but started instead that peculiar New World institution—the plantation.

Historians say there was a dwindling interest in slavery in the South about the time of the American Revolution. But in the decade that followed, two events planted slavery firmly upon the Southland: the development of sea-island cotton, and the invention of the cotton gin. The new cotton was a long-fibered variety that could be grown on the lowlands. And the gin—while only a simple device for separating the seeds from the fibers—caused the demand for cotton to soar by rendering it cheap.

More and more acres were planted, and more and more slaves were needed to plant and pick. Slavery was again "necessary."

Meanwhile, out west the hacienda was not dead but only sleeping. When the United States acquired the California Territory from Mexico, the land was still divided into large

Water for forty families in a migrant camp.

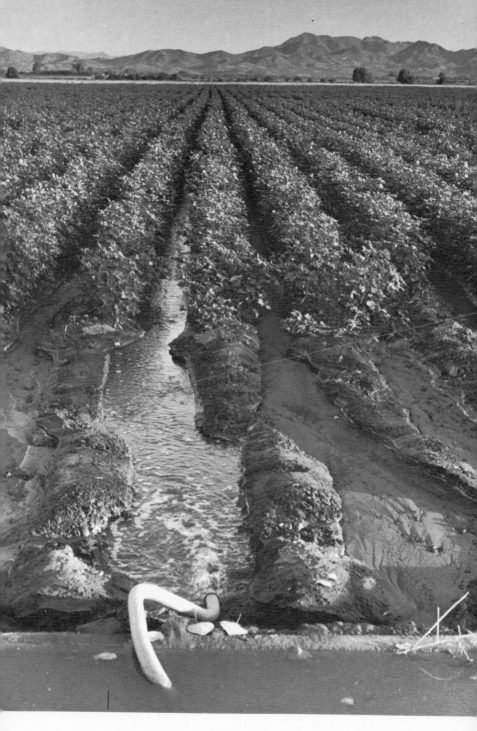

Water for the crops.

Helicopter spraying crops near Delano, California. The crop duster is approaching field workers at extreme right of picture. (Between 1950 and 1961, 3,040 farm workers were poisoned in California by pesticides and other farm chemicals. Twenty-two workers and sixty-three children died.)

Norman Smith,
organizer for AWOC.

Cesar Chavez, of the
Farm Workers Association.

Rev. Jack Mansfield and the staff of the Rocking Horse. (*Left to right*) Frank Rush, Rev. Mansfield, Polly Richards, Georgie Hughes.

An old Arkansas tenant shack, deserted when five small farms were combined to make one big farm. The displaced sharecroppers and tenants are absorbed into the migrant streams.

Rural slums, like this one in the San Joaquin Valley, are the new homes for migrants escaping the stream. Often outside the city limits, the rural slum is without water, police and fire protection, schools, and garbage disposal service. Living conditions are worse than in the migrant camps.

Symbol of migrancy—an old bus turned into a home.

Rusting car bodies in a cabin yard. Many of the residents of this California rural slum are Negroes who were brought out in the 1920's to work in cotton; others are recent arrivals, who came as migrants but found life in the Golden West the same as down home.

holdings. Many of the first American settlers were able to
get the deeds to these vast empires by conniving with or
bribing the Mexican governors. By the time most young
men took Horace Greeley's advice and went west, it was
too late. When California was annexed, most of the good
land west of the Coast Range mountains, and the lower
Sacramento and San Joaquin valleys, had been taken.

In a single decade (1836–1846) Mexican governors
handed over 700 haciendas. About 800 Americans thus acquired over 8,000,000 acres of land.

Many of the Spanish grants were illegal. Some were out-
right frauds. Some were of that borderline legality typical
of the period. A man named Limantour, armed with a bogus
Mexican grant, claimed the entire city of San Francisco,
and supposedly almost got it.

One of the most famous land-grabbers was a German
immigrant named Henry Miller. He got off the boat in
1847 with $6.00 in his pocket. He proceeded to build an
empire roughly the size of Belgium. It stretched across the
whole Southwest. At the height of his glory he boasted,
with truth, that he could ride from Canada to Mexico and
spend every night on one of his own ranches.

The tactics he used to get his land were imaginative, if
not wholly admirable. Swamp lands were open to claim at
the time. Miller hitched a team of horses to a boat and
crossed the vast tract of desirable land. He then claimed
it under the "swamp land" laws. He solemnly testified
that he himself had crossed the land in a boat. (Miller's bi-
ographer denied this, but such methods were typical of the
period.)

The first known migrant-worker route wound through
the Miller empire. He encouraged tramps and hobos to pass
through his territory so he could put them to work in the
fields at harvest. The route they traveled came to be known
as the Dirty Plate Route, after instructions Miller gave, in
writing, to all his foremen:

"Never refuse a tramp a meal, but never give him more than one meal. A tramp should be a tramp and keep on tramping. Never let the tramps eat with the other men. Make them wait until the men are through, and then make them eat off the same plates."*

Miller also made it a practice to hand out small coins to the tramps and hobos he passed on the street. He died in 1916, believing himself to be a much-loved man.

By the time of the Civil War, the big wheat farms had developed in California. Using the steam tractor and gangs of "hobo" labor, they became the protoypes of the modern factory farm.

Henry George, the noted economist, observed in 1871 that "California is not a country of farms but a country of plantations and estates. Agriculture is speculation." Labor was furnished by the "bindle stiffs"—tramps.

"And over our ill-kept, shadeless, dusty roads, where a house is an unwonted landmark, and which run frequently for miles through the same man's land, plod the tramps, with blanket on back, the laborers of the California farmer, looking for work, in its seasons, or toiling back to the city when the ploughing is done or the wheat crop is gathered."

During this time the roadbeds had been hacked through the mountains. East and West were linked together at Promontory Summit, Utah, on May 10, 1869. And the thousands of Chinese coolies who had built the Central (now Southern) Pacific railroad were released upon the labor market.

In swift order the western haciendas were supplied with cheap Chinese labor from the railroads. And new markets opened up in the East. Not only did the railroad connect the eastern markets and the western fields, but greatly accelerated the growth of the West. Food demand rose sharply.

For a time there was a kind of "golden age" in California

* Carey McWilliams, *Factories in the Field.*

farming. In 1880, 90 percent of the field labor was done by the railroad coolies.

An article in *Sunset* magazine described it: "The grower looked over his goodly acres, calculated his crop and went to his Chinese labor boss. 'John,' he would say, 'you find me fifty men. Come Thursday.'

"The square brown man would consider the question and say, 'All lite [sic], I get 'em' . . . and there you were. Thursday next, fifty replicas of John would appear with mess kit and such bedding as they needed. They lived in the fields, worked as the locusts, cleared the crop and melted away."

Two years later some of the gold of the age rubbed off. Organized labor resented the flood of cheap coolie labor. As a result the Chinese Exclusion Act was passed, and the coolies came no more.

Some of the growers turned to the South. One wrote in the *Pacific Rural Express:* "As the South has tens of thousands of Negroes who can barely make a living, we conceived the idea of contracting for Negro help . . . and shipping them out to take the place of the Chinese . . ."

But this plan was never fully exploited. They found something even better. A new oriental encomienda was recruited from rural Japan. By 1910 there were over 72,000 Japanese on the factory farms of the West. They were expert farmers themselves and masters at developing orchards and vineyards on land considered worthless. They introduced rice, new plant varieties, and improved existing ones.

They were quick and efficient workers, and a source of valuable information. They were unbelievably cheap, quickly outbidding any competing crews.

Disenchantment with the Japanese came very soon. After dominating the labor market, they began to ask for higher wages.

To make matters worse, they even started to buy land

of their own. Although they had to buy the poorest land, they somehow managed to make crops grow on it.

The big growers, like the conquistadors, were looking for a cheap labor source. The Japanese were welcome only as long as they knew their place. Consequently, Japanese immigration was "stabilized" in 1913 by the so-called Gentlemen's Agreement. The California legislature—dominated then, as now, by the growers—passed the Alien Land Law. Under this curious law, later declared unconstitutional, the land owned by the Japanese was simply confiscated.

A new face, reddish brown this time, replaced the yellow man. It was 1914. The guns of revolution sounded in Mexico. The guns of war sounded in Europe. From Mexico came droves of peasants, driven from their homes in the revolution. From Europe came a cry for food in wartime. Once more, new sources of cheap labor obligingly appeared along with new demands for food.

Some of the Mexicans came as legal immigrants. But as many as 80 percent were illegal "wetbacks." Uneasy about their contraband labor, growers began to look across the sea. Ten thousand Hindustani came to California, and the Filipino population rose to 30,500. The Filipinos too started to demand more wages, and the bulk of the work shifted to the Mexicans.

After World War I had ended and the revolution in Mexico was settled, the wetback refugees began to drift homeward. The coming Depression was being felt. Wages were so low that the Southwest held little attraction for the Mexican worker.

The migrant drama caught the nation's attention in the thirties. Great dust storms swept the plains and dimmed the sun as far away as the East Coast. Long lines of tenant families—the Gasoline Gypsies—crossed the desert into

California looking for work. The dust bowl refugees were only one set of characters in the migrant epic that began long before the Joads of *The Grapes of Wrath*.

By 1934 the Anglo population in the labor camps reached 50 percent. As the bitter years of dust storms and Depression set in, Okies and Arkies continued to stream into California in caravans of jalopies.

It was ironic that after so many years of coolies and peons, American workers took over in a time of widespread unemployment. Hence, wages and working conditions, bad as they were, got worse. For every job that was open, there was a hungry carload of migrants. Men fought in the field over a row of beans.

For the first time western growers admitted there was a labor surplus. The Farm Security Administration reported that by 1938, 221,000 dust bowlers had entered California.

With the coming of the Second World War, shipyards and aircraft industries drained off the surplus labor left by the draft board. Food demands climbed to their usual wartime levels. Another source of cheap labor had to be found.

The government was induced to sanction the wetbacks. And in 1944 the United States spent nearly $24 million to supply the growers with 62,170 braceros.

As the war progressed, prisoners of war were turned over to growers, along with convicts. Japanese-Americans, impounded in concentration camps, were released to the custody of the big growers. Armed guards patrolled the fields. When the war ended the POW's went back to Italy and Germany, and the convicts went back to their cells.

The wetbacks remained, and their questionable legal position became more and more evident. Border patrols, on orders from Washington, looked the other way during the harvest season, and the wetbacks streamed in. The federal government not only condoned wetback traffic during the harvest season, but actually encouraged it. In 1951 the President's Commission studying the problems of migratory labor discovered this incredible situation:

> . . . wetbacks [who were apprehended] were given identification slips in the United States by the Immigration and Naturalization Service, which entitled them, within a few minutes, to step back across the border and become contract workers. There was no other way to obtain the indispensable slip of paper except to be found illegally in the United States. Thus violators of law were rewarded by receiving legal contracts while the same opportunities were denied law-abiding citizens of Mexico. The United States, having engaged in a program giving preference in contracting to those who had broken the law, had encouraged violation of the immigration laws. *Our government thus has become a contributor to the growth of an illegal traffic which it has the responsibility to prevent* [italics added].

In 1950, when the "police action" began in Korea, President Truman had appointed a commission to study the problems of migrant labor. The pressure was building up for more cheap labor to meet the anticipated new demands for food.

Following completion of the report of the President's Commission, the Eighty-second Congress, on July 12, 1951, passed Public Law 78. The commission had recommended a few months earlier that "no special measures be adopted to increase the number of alien contract workers beyond the number admitted in 1950." In 1952 the McCarran-Walter Act (Public Law 414) was passed over the President's veto. (This was a new immigration and naturalization act, which permitted the temporary importation of foreign labor under contract for periods up to three years.)

In 1951, 192,000 legal braceros came in under contract

to work in the fields of the Southwest. Illegal wetback traffic began to decline. But by the end of the decade the number of braceros had risen far above the wartime emergency levels of either World War II or the Korean War. In 1959 there were 437,000 Mexican nationals scattered across the United States from Texas to Michigan.

The development of migratory labor on the East Coast was much less complicated. The plantations of the South were shattered, as if a giant hammer had been brought down upon a land of glass. The plantation-slave economy fragmented into the sharecropper and tenant economy.

From the South was taken. To the West was given. Whatever was bad about southern farming the tenants and croppers made worse. The soil was exhausted. King Cotton, overthrown in the Civil War, fled west. In 1821 South Carolina and Georgia grew half the cotton. By 1850 Alabama led, and South Carolina was a poor fourth. By 1900 the center was in Texas.

Charleston saw its bright future fade. Many thought it destined to be a greater port than New York. Unable to meet western competition. South Carolina saw its land values decline as the centers of trade slowly moved to New Orleans and Mobile.

The South was a patchwork of small, poor farms. But big farms were sprouting now in the North. The first migrant stream, the eastern equivalent of the Dirty Plate Route, began some time in the late 1800's.

"No one knows how long migratory labor has been moving up and down the Atlantic seaboard. The Industrial Commission noted in 1901 . . . that colored labor from the South was being used in the New England States. A grower testified that most of the fruit in Connecticut was picked by Negroes, with as many as 260 and 300 workers being imported every year from Georgia, South Carolina, and Florida. For years prior to 1901, Negroes were imported each season by steamers from Norfolk to Rhode Island to work in the fruit and vegetable fields."*

It was not until 1920 that the East Coast migrant stream developed the pattern of today. In that year, thousands of acres of black gold—rich muckland—were opened up in the Florida glades. With a year-round subtropical climate, three or four crops could be grown and harvested each year. Now a man could work the winter in Florida, the summer in the Middle Atlantic States, and the early autumn in the North.

East and West had at last met. On both coasts, big commercial farms dominated, and a shifting labor force came when it was called, and left when the work was done.

In 1950 a new tomato variety was developed in Florida, and the limestone pinelands were suitable for its growth. The demand for labor increased. Where the West had turned to Mexico and the Orient, the South turned to the offshore islands: Puerto Rico and the West Indies.

Every time agribusiness has needed more labor, it has been able to tap new reserves abroad. Wages and working conditions have thus been left begging. And the farm family, trying to match the commercial farm's gangs of cheap labor, has been driven to the wall.

* Carey McWilliams, *op. cit.*

7

STRANGERS IN OUR FIELDS

We depend on misfortune to build up our force of migratory
workers and when the supply is low because there is not enough
misfortune at home, we rely on misfortune abroad to replenish
the supply.

—*Report of the President's*
Commission on Migratory Labor

EACH YEAR a quarter of a million workers from Mexico,
the West Indies, Canada, and Japan enter the United States
to work in the harvest.

Public Law 78, the Korean War emergency measure, has
been extended again and again, expiring this time on December
31, 1964. Under this law, American growers brought
in contract labor from Mexico for short periods of work.

Public Law 414, passed a year later, in 1952, remains in
effect. Under this law, growers may bring in foreign work-

ers from periods of thirty days to three years. In 1962, an average year, growers employed 1,200 Japanese, 125 Filipinos, 13,000 British West Indians, and 8,700 Canadians under Public Law 414. Over 180,000 Mexicans came in under Public Law 78. And 13,526 Americans from Puerto Rico came in under direct contract.

In addition to these workers, two other groups of workers have appeared in recent years under provisions of Public Law 414. The distinction between the two groups is often confused. They are called "blue-carders" and "green-carders."

The blue-carder is a commuter. He lives in Mexico and works in the United States. His blue-colored visa is good for only 72 hours. About 1,200 blue-carders a day go in and out of the Imperial Valley of Southern California. The number seems to be much greater, but there are many Mexican-Americans—that is, United States citizens—who live in Mexico and commute to the valley.

Blue-carders also commute from Mexico to the southern regions of Arizona, New Mexico, and Texas. As a result, the biggest source of the domestic migrant stream is out of Texas. It is fed by the domestic farm workers displaced by the cheaper labor of the blue-card commuters and the braceros. These dislocated Texas-Mexicans head for Minnesota, Idaho, Michigan, and other states to find work. This explains the seeming paradox that Texas is both *the largest user and exporter of migrant labor*. The Mexicans come in and the Americans leave.

The green-carder is an immigrant alien who enters the United States under the usual quota system and the provisions of Public Law 414. While the blue visa is for *temporary* admission, the green visa is for *permanent* admission to the United States. The Secretary of Labor decides whether more workers are needed in the area in which the prospective immigrant intends to live (and in the occupation he intends to follow). In other words, the immigrant states what his occupation is and where he intends to live. The Secretary of Labor admits him or bars him on this basis.

The fallacy is immediately obvious. The United States is not a police state. Once in the country as a resident alien, the green-carder is not obligated to go where he intended, or to engage in his stated occupation.

The effect of PL 414 is frequently changed by "rulings" handed down by the Labor Department. Until recently the Labor Department—supposedly prodded by the State Department—examined green-carder applications only if 25 or more were being offered jobs by a single employer.

Facing a cutoff of the bracero program, growers immediately began importing green-card workers from Mexico in groups of 24. Used-car dealers were hiring "car salesmen" from Mexico two dozen at a time—and turning them over to the grower associations for a fee. There was a thriving black market in green-carders. An executive of a big western growers' association said they were importing green-carders as fast as they could.

In 1963, however, the Labor Department slowed down the green-carder influx with another "ruling." Henceforth they are to consider each application separately instead of only examining groups of 25.

No one knows how many of the green-carders are employed in agriculture. In 1959 there were 191,305 Mexican aliens in California (including diplomats and braceros). In two years the figure jumped to 219,335, an increase of 28,000. In 1962 the *California Farm Reporter* claimed there were 30,000 to 35,000 green-carders in the state, and in 1963 estimates ran to 41,000.

The green-carder poses a greater threat to domestic labor conditions than the bracero. Unprotected in an alien land, the poorly educated are easily taken advantage of. It is frequently reported that many growers illegally collect all the green visas and hold them until the end of the season. Without his visa, the alien worker is afraid to leave his job lest he be deported—not a groundless fear, by the way.

Not all green-carders stay in the field. The Giannini Foundation at the University of California started a survey of these workers. (The foundation was endowed by the Bank of America and is generally considered to be the voice of agribusiness.) The report was not completed because it was "too explosive," according to Eric Thor. It became evident that less than 5 percent of the new workers interviewed intended to stay at their farm job. Many were educated, skilled workers who used the field work only as a means of entering the country. Asked if growers were aware that they were adding to the overcrowded domestic labor market, Dr. Thor replied, "Well, growers aren't concerned with that. They are only interested in this year's crop."

The laborer's only value lies in the work he can perform. And granting or withholding his labor is the only bargaining power he has. However, when a domestic farm worker withholds his labor, the grower claims a labor shortage and is allowed to use cheap foreign labor. So the American worker moves on, perhaps to the next valley, the next state, or another section of the country.

The greatest single obstacle to the way of improving the lot of the American farm worker is the annual inundation of the "strangers in our fields."

The bracero enters and leaves the United States through reception stations along the border. Here they await the fleets of buses and trucks that shuttle them back and forth between the company farms of the North and the border. A federal employee in one of these centers described a scene he witnessed one afternoon:

"I went to the front office to find out how many men were to be fed for supper. About ten minutes after five I saw Arnold Edge drive the Labor Department's pickup to the front door. Edge is a transportation assistant at the Reception Center.

"He grabbed a bracero by the arms, from behind, and

walked him, you might say, around to the truck. Edge opened the door and told the bracero to get in. The bracero said, in Spanish, 'No, I'm not going.' Then Edge picked him up bodily and tried to shove him into the cab. But the man spread his hands and feet in such a way that Edge couldn't do it.

"Edge reached around from in back and hit him in the face. Then he hit him at least once more. I didn't count the times he hit him.

"Bob came out and tried to help Edge. They succeeded except for one foot, which the bracero wedged between the windshield post and the door—in the hinge. Then a man named Sam Williams, who represents several farmers' associations, came by. He went over to the truck and attempted to free the foot that the bracero had wedged in the door. They were having trouble—that boy was small, but he was wiry. To make him let loose, Edge struck him right in the face with his elbow. The blow was so hard that it jerked the bracero's head backward, and it smashed the window in the back of the cab.

"They got the foot loose. They shoved him into the middle of the seat and drove off. They were bound for the border, but I don't know what happened after that.

"Later I found that the man had broken a collarbone on the job and had been awarded a five-hundred-dollar judgment. When the man arrived at the Reception Center he was asked to sign a statement saying that he had received two hundred dollars, and was told that the other three hundred would be sent to him after he returned to Mexico. He complained that he wanted to wait for the whole five hundred dollars. He was advised to sign. He refused.

"After the truck got back from the border, some of the employees at the center saw blood on the upholstery. Edge said the bracero had cut his finger."

This was the way one of the 200,000 Mexicans who worked on American farms went home. The scene was described to Henry Anderson, of the Agricultural Workers

Organizing Committee, by an employee of the El Centro, California, Reception Center, through which braceros are funneled on their way to the farms of California and Arizona.

"It is a shame," said another employee in the same camp, "the way people at the Center treat the braceros. Everybody curses the braceros and shoves them around. Right now they have a couple of young bullies in the photography section. If a bracero doesn't hold his head just the way they want him to, they give him judo chops across the neck, or grab him by the hair and shake him or even bang his head against the wall. I saw them bang one man's head against the wall three times so hard I thought it would break open. He had something wrong with his neck and couldn't hold his head straight was why they got so mad.

"The cursing is terrible. I heard one bracero ask, 'Where do I go now?' The immigration man, instead of telling him where the next barracks was, said, *Vete a la chingada!* This means 'go screw yourself.'

"Another thing you hear over and over again is *hijo de la chingada*, which means something like 'son of a whore.' It is a very bad thing to say in Mexico because they feel very strong about their mothers. In Mexico a man might even kill another man for saying this. But in the Reception Center you hear it all the time from these young guys.

"I have even seen a lot of braceros cry after they were talked to in this way. And it takes a lot to make a Mexican man cry."

The bracero program has been declared by its proponents as "a uniquely successful foreign aid program" which gives the Mexicans a chance to earn money and be exposed to the American way of life. Mexicans describe the bracero program somewhat differently. "We were forced to accept contracts in the Imperial Valley. We worked three days. Out of these seven men, I was the one who earned the most —forty-one cents. Another man made twenty-six cents."

"When it came time to pay us," said another bracero,

"there was *puro trinquete* ('much swindling'). Some of the men had *la suerte más volteada* ('bad luck') and hardly earned any money at all."

"There is no use going to work," said a third man. "We do not make any money anyway. When we weigh in the cotton, instead of deducting four pounds for the sack, they deduct ten. They cheat us."

Wages are always bad. But one of the bitterest complaints of the foreign workers has been over the food. A San Joaquin grower, Fred Van Dyke, has taken a greater interest in the seasonal workers than his fellow growers. Bracero feeding, he claims, is nothing but a racket. A gregarious and outspoken Presbyterian Republican, Van Dyke has often stirred the ire of the growers in the valley. "I know personally of men who have grown wealthy feeding braceros for the grower associations. Braceros are charged a dollar seventy-five a day for their meals, which doesn't sound like much. But some of the big camps have a thousand men. This means a gross income of seventeen hundred and fifty dollars a day.

"Now they buy beans by the sack, and rice too—right from the warehouse. And for meat they use tripe. At sixteen cents a pound it's the cheapest you can get. Well, they can keep a man alive for about seventy-five cents to a dollar a day. Depends on what you feed him. Cheap hamburger is about thirty cents a pound. Might put some of that in the beans now and then. Well, they make about seven hundred and fifty to a thousand dollars a day feeding braceros."

Foreign workers come to the United States, as a Mexican consul put it, "to get the almighty dollar. It often turns out to be the all-flighty dollar." But in spite of the miseries of life on the harvest trail, they still come by the thousands. This has prompted growers to conclude that regardless of the hardships the foreigner encounters on our native soil, "it's better than what they had at home," and few growers lose much sleep over the field labor's problems.

Over the years growers have shown a decided preference for the foreign farm workers. The reasons are many. Very often the foreigner does not speak English. He is uninformed about his rights and in a poor position to defend them if they are violated. He is willing to work for less and under poorer conditions. Imported farm workers are always single males. Housing and transportation are simpler. And when the farmer has done with them, they can be shipped back where they came from—if any of them make trouble, they can be shipped home a little earlier.

Foreign workers can be used only when there is a shortage of domestic workers. The definition of a legitimate labor shortage is therefore a prime issue.

The yellowed and dusty pages of back issues of the conservative Los Angeles *Times* tell a strange story. "Farm Outlook Dim" read a headline on May 17, 1936. "Scarcity of Labor Dominant in Farm Labor Problem" headlined the *Times* on April 4 of the next year. And on September 22, 1940: "Cotton Picker Shortage Seen." All this, of course, was during a time when California was being inundated with Okies and Arkies.

A different set of headlines during this same period (also from the Los Angeles *Times*) gives what was undoubtedly a truer picture. "Pea Pickers Flood State," in 1936. "Migratory Labor Nearing Saturation Point," in 1937. "Steps Taken to Avert Cotton Picker Influx," in 1938. And in 1940: "Farm Surplus Grows."

In 1950 the *Times* announced "100 Children Reported Starving in Migratory Farm Labor Camp." And the same year there was a "Shortage of Field Workers."

In 1954, while "San Joaquin Valley Jobless Farm Labor Seeks Surplus Food," there was a "Picker Shortage."

In 1958, when "Record 445,000 Mexican Nationals [were] Used on U.S. Farms," there were, a year later, "Stranded Farm Workers, Hungry, Homeless."

Shortage of workers amid mass unemployment, foreign workers in record numbers while American workers can't find jobs—these are long-standing contradictions in farm labor. Growers say they can't find workers. Workers say they can't find jobs.

Part of the paradox lies in the definition of the terms. A shortage of labor exists for many growers when they don't have more than twice the number of workers they can get by with. Extra hands keep the wages down and the union out.

The worker's idea of the proper labor supply is when he can choose between jobs.

The theory of the laws that enable growers to import labor was that both worker and grower would benefit. In practice these laws crushed the worker and gave the grower an almost limitless supply of cheap labor.

The topsy-turvy logic of Public Law 78 is worthy of closer examination. Briefly, it said that if a grower cannot attract enough domestic labor at the prevailing wages, he can get Mexican nationals—the presence of whom shall have no adverse effect on local labor.

An analogy to this has been made, called Public Law 78-A. Under this tongue-in-cheek "law," all housewives would get together and decide how much they could pay for groceries. If they cannot find enough food at the prices they have decided to pay, the housewives' association notifies the Secretary of Agriculture that there is a food shortage. He then imports cheaper foreign food. But this is to have no adverse effect on the neighborhood stores.

Obviously, when a worker refuses a job at 35 cents an hour (the prevailing wage for field workers in Arkansas, which has used as many as 40,000 braceros annually), he only makes it possible for the grower to get Mexicans.

An interesting example of the law in action was the shifting wages in the Imperial Valley. For many years domestic workers in the winter lettuce harvest were paid a piece rate of a penny a head. This worked out to an hourly wage of from $1.25 to $2.00—good money for harvesting.

As growers began to use more braceros, the piece rate

was finally dropped and the wage level in the valley fell. For several years, prior to 1961, it was frozen at about 70 cents an hour. When President Kennedy signed the extention of Public Law 78 in 1961 (for two years), he instructed the Secretary of Labor to see to it that the program have no adverse effect on domestic labor.

As a result, Imperial Valley growers who sought to use braceros were instructed to reinstate the old piece rate of a penny a head. (It can be noted in passing that if harvest wages were doubled, i.e., at a piece rate of 2 cents a head, consumer prices should not be seriously affected.)

In anticipation of this change, growers had increased the hourly wage from 70 cents to $1. But as soon as the Labor Department called for the old piece rate, two hundred growers flew to Washington to protest. The department backed down and agreed that the growers could pay either $1 an hour *or* the piece rate of 24 cents a carton. *The choice was to be left to the worker.* That the growers were satisfied with the new arrangement indicated that they didn't intend for the workers, most of whom were braceros, to have much say in the matter after all.

And the nature of the choice—between $1 an hour or $2 an hour—indicated that the Department of Labor was either naïve or cynical.

The mystery was cleared up when Mrs. Elizabeth Longenbohn, an accountant employed by an El Centro lettuce company, announced that she had falsified the payroll records.

What Mrs. Longenbohn had done, on the orders of the company owners, was pad the hours reported by the labor crews. This lowered, on paper, the hourly wage. Thus, the Labor Department was unaware of what the piece-rate earnings actually were. Apparently the wage surveyors had asked the growers what they were paying. But no one bothered to ask the workers what they were earning.

If it had been discovered that the piece rate was equal to

$2 an hour, then the bracero hourly wage of $1 would have to be doubled. It would have been clear that the use of the Mexicans had definitely had an adverse effect on wages in the valley.

"In March [1962]," said Mrs. Longenbohn, "a representative of the Department of Labor inspected my books and complimented me on them. I must assume from this that *my records showed no discrepancies with those of other bookkeepers keeping records on the lettuce harvest and that they were, therefore, all false* [italics added]."

When the lettuce company moved to Arizona for the harvest there, she offered to help the Arizona accountant set up the piece rates. The general manager replied that they weren't paying piece rates any more. "The braceros have a choice of one dollar an hour or the piece rate. We are going to take to Arizona only the ones who want a dollar an hour. They don't want to go home [to Mexico], so they'll take the dollar an hour and that will end the piece rate, because what they choose here establishes our payment."

The advantage to the grower of using braceros is clear. Subtle schemes have been worked out to get rid of domestic workers when their presence threatens to discount a "labor shortage."

In one town the local growers and the Farm Placement Service had a system going whereby a domestic worker was required to register every morning in order to work that day. He had to get a "referral card" from the Farm Placement Office which opened at eight in the morning. By the time the worker got to the farm, the buses (loaded with braceros) had left for the fields. In fact, they had left at seven, which made getting a job impossible. The grower's foreman would smile and say, "Come back tomorrow. We've finished hiring today."

One ranch foreman who defected to a labor union told

how he used to get rid of domestic workers. "If a busload managed to get hired, I let them wait for an hour or so on the bus. Then I'd drive them to the 'wrong' field and let them pick for twenty minutes.

"I'd discover my mistake and load them up and drive them to another field. This would be a poor field ready for second picking. If anybody complained, I'd fire them right there. We'd waste most of the morning. In the early afternoon I'd say that was all we wanted picked today. After a couple of days of this they wouldn't come back, because they couldn't make any money."

One domestic worker who struggled with this system wrote a graphic letter to a labor union, addressed "To Anyone Who Cares."

My name is Rafael. I have six children and a wife, which makes eight with me.

For the last two years we have been traveling from California to Arizona, barely living and taking all kinds of insults from the foremen. They do this with the intention of getting us disgusted so we leave our jobs, but we stand fast and take all this for the sake of our children.

We beg the foreman not to take our jobs away, that we have many children, but the foreman tells us this: "It is not my fault for you to have so many children for your pleasure. I'm only interested in the work. The company don't care about things of that sort; besides, the company has plenty of braceros and actually is not interested in local workers because they are very lazy and don't want to work."

Then we go home and on the way we pick up some cabbage and carrots and with this we arrive home. Next we go to see the owner of the little store in the corner and we explain our problems to him and soften his heart for our children. He gives us food on credit.

The next week we go to see the same man with some excuse, and again he gives us food on credit. The third week he wrinkles his nose, and when the fourth week comes we leave at midnight to some other town. We leave at this hour so the owner of the house we rent will not notice because we are two months behind.

When we get to the other town we find ourselves with the same problems, and again we start all over again doing the same we done before in the town we just left. If one of our kids gets sick we take him to the county hospital if we are lucky, but most of the time we treat them with herbs, baking soda, or with lard.

But we get behind, so we have to move again without paying the rent. We always go to some town where nobody knows us and this is the way we pass our lives.

My wish is to get a good week's pay so I can afford to buy my children some cakes or something sweet, because I know that all children enjoy these things. But the way things are now it seems to me that there is going to come a day when we will not be able to live any place, since we owe money in all places we have been and fear also the police might be looking for us.

There are thousands of families with our same problems. But we have courage and will take it.

There are hundreds of "atrocity stories," as the growers call them, like this. And they all tell of the same frustration.

Documentation abounds to prove what logic tells us. No industry can be a healthy one as long as it is hooked on what Van Dyke calls the "peon labor jag." Foreign-labor programs must be stopped and no rebirth of the bracero system must be allowed under a new name.

8

THE INTEGRATORS

And now the great owners and the companies invented a new method. A great owner bought a cannery. And when the peaches and the pears were ripe he cut the price of fruit below the cost of raising it. And as cannery owner he paid himself a low price for the fruit and kept the price of canned goods up and took his profit. And the little farmers who owned no canneries lost their farms, and they were taken by the great owners, the banks, and the companies who also owned the canneries. As time went on, there were fewer farms. The little farmers moved into town for a while and exhausted their credit, exhausted their friends, their relatives. And then they too went on the highways. And the roads were crowded with men ravenous for work, murderous for work.

JOHN STEINBECK, *The Grapes of Wrath*

ONE STEAMING JULY AFTERNOON, Leland Duval, farm editor of the Little Rock *Arkansas Gazette* set aside his work to talk about egg money, chickens, and farms. Like most observers of contemporary farming, Duval has watched with apprehension as the American farm has become a factory. What happens to the farm will determine what happens to migrant labor.

Farming is moving toward "vertical integration." "The best way to explain it," said Duval, "is in the poultry industry, where the process is almost complete. Out in the grain belt, the farmer's wife used to raise chickens. She fed them on the grain and sold the eggs to roving truckers. By the time these eggs got to Arkansas, they weren't too good. Chicken was the same way. And the price was high.

"Customers were demanding something better. After the war a lot of men came home and decided to raise chickens. They used their GI loans, built some coops, bought the chicks, and the American Dream came true. They were in business for themselves. And business was good. Production cost was thirty cents a pound and the chickens sold for thirty-five cents a pound. If the price started to drop, the GI poultry farmer cut his production, and it went back up.

"Business was so good that a lot of other people decided to get in on it. During this time some remarkable developments were going on. The growing cycle was cut from twelve to eight weeks. Feed and breeding stock were improved. All this caused overproduction. And the price fell.

"But that was all right. Production costs fell, too. The housewife could now get better chicken for less money. She bought plenty. [In 1945 the average American ate five pounds of broiler meat. Today he eats twenty-eight.]

"Within a few years the chickens, you might say, really came home to roost. The selling price dropped to production cost. There was no profit.

"When the feed-store man heard about this, he offered the poultry farmer a deal. 'You keep producing at cost, and I'll pay you a nickel for every chicken. It'll come out of my feed profit, but I'd rather lose some than all.'

"This new arrangement lasted until prices fell again, and this time both the chicken farmer and the feed-store man called it quits.

"Now the feed mill stepped in. It offered to subsidize the feed store if the feed store would continue to subsidize the farmer. But before very long the feed mill went directly to the farmer. Almost overnight, the feed stores all over America went out of business.*

"The margin between selling price and cost was still thin. The feed mill next bought out the hatcheries and the processors. They even started making their own medicines. For a time they ran retail stores.

"In the meantime, the poultry farmer is still getting a nickel a chicken. The more chickens, the more nickels. He stopped caring about the market long ago. I remember visiting a friend of mine who raises chickens. We were going fishing. The man's son went out and killed six chickens to cut up for bait. I asked him if he didn't think that was rather expensive bait. He said no, because his father only got a nickel a chicken, and he figured thirty cents wasn't too much to pay for bait.

"The GI who came home from the war to start his own

* "Pillsbury Mills did not market a single broiler prior to 1960. Beginning in 1953, however, Pillsbury began to take notice of the rise in broiler production in Alabama. As this surveillance continued, the company saw the state's production increase from 28 million to 102 million in 1957, at which point it became the fourth largest poultry-producing state in the country. In 1958 Pillsbury elected to construct production facilities in Alabama. At the time, the company ascertained that the bulk of the broilers within the state were being produced by about 40 persons or concerns. Of these 40, 20 were eliminated as potential customers either because they made their own feed or because they were satisfied with competing feed manufacturers. By 1960, when Alabama production reached 176 million broilers, Pillsbury opened its mill, only to discover that its potential customers had dropped to 10 because of the growing integration in the industry. And by 1960 potential customers were down to five. Because of this reduced market potential, Pillsbury commenced its own broiler-growing operation through the use of contract growers in an effort to make its new facilities profitable." "Small Business Problems in the Poultry Industry" hearings before the Special Subcommittee of the Select Committee on Small Business, House of Representatives, January 3, 1963.

business now finds himself with a seventy-five-dollar-a-week, eighty-hour job. And he is always in hock to the bank or the feed mill to finance his next bunch of chicks. Not all the farmers get a nickel any more. The grain company has a formula for efficiency. They take the number of chickens that reach the market and compare it with the amount of grain used. The farmer is paid on this rating.

"Grain is delivered by the ton. The farmer has no way of measuring it. And he has no way of knowing how many of the chickens lived to reach the market. He has to take the company's word for everything.

"Imagine the farmer pondering this when the grain is delivered. He gets into a chat with the truck driver—lo and behold, he discovers the truck driver makes a hundred bucks a week, works eight hours a day, and doesn't owe anyone a dime. He begins to wonder if he isn't being had."

A similar story is told in farming except for the fact that the row-crop farmer has labor to squeeze. Many farmers, like Fred Van Dyke, are convinced that cheap gang labor is hastening the demise of the family farmer. He says:

"A man from a big tomato-packing house, or a big grape-shipping firm, or a big asparagus cannery comes up to me and says, 'How much you got in the ground so far?' Figuring land preparation, seeds, fertilizer, irrigation, insecticides, and everything else, I tell him, 'Oh, about ten thousand dollars.' He says, 'All right. I'll pay you fifteen thousand for your crop as she sits. You don't have to worry about picking or selling a thing. You want a check? I'll write you a check right now.' I say, 'Well, I don't know. I ought to be able to get four hundred dollars an acre out of it. That would be eighteen thousand dollars.' He says, 'Maybe. But look at the chances you'll be taking.' I think of my taxes that are due and the bank payment coming up next month. With fifteen thousand dollars I'll be in the clear. Without it, I'll have to try to get a crop loan. I weigh the peace of mind against the added profit I might make if the crop turns out to be a good one and the market holds up. After a minute or two I say, 'Oh, to heck with it. Give me the check.'

"When harvest time comes around, the packing company brings in a big crew of braceros, packs my green tomatoes or whatever it is, right there in the field, sends them off to market, moves its crew of braceros to the field of the next 'farmer' it has contracted with, and so on. I'm not really a farmer any more under those conditions. I have rented my land and my tomato plants to somebody else. Why? Because that somebody else has a captive labor force I can't compete with.

"The profits which these vertical integrators are making today (and in many cases, believe me, they are handsome profits) should properly be going to the farmers themselves. They *would* be going to farmers—*if* my friends and I were better organized among ourselves, and *if* we weren't forced to compete with the captive labor crews of the vertical integrators.

"Take away the shippers' and packers' and canneries' task forces of braceros and we would be on a more nearly even footing. It might look as though Di Giorgio Fruit Corporation and California Packing Corporation will always have competitive advantages over me. But in some respects, *they* can't compete with *me*. I know more about growing tomatoes or grapes than the agribusiness men and their mercenaries do."

Unfortunately, the small and middle-size farmers like Van Dyke are being driven from the land, regardless of how much they know about growing tomatoes. To the vertically integrated farm, food is simply raw material. An ordinary farmer is no match.

Witness the California Packing Corporation, known to consumers by the Del Monte label. CalPac owns 24,000 acres and leases 74,000. It has 29 subsidiaries spread from South Africa to Alaska. It owns 44 canneries, 7 can-making plants, 5 seed-processing plants, 3 seed-experiment stations, 3 dried-fruit plants. In addition to this it owns a vinegar works, a shipping terminal, a fresh asparagus packing plant, a label-printing shop, an apricot pit-and-kernel plant, a cherry-barreling plant, 5 laboratories, and 50 warehouses throughout the United States and Canada. CalPac has assets of over $260 million and its sales run in excess of $350 million.

Another integrated "farmer," the Kern County Land Company, has holdings twice the size of Rhode Island. The Di Giorgio Fruit Corporation (S & W label) has 19,000 acres in California and 5,400 in Florida. In Arizona, the *average* grower-shipper invests $600,000 a year to grow, pack, and ship his crop.

As the little farmer goes, so goes the little store. The A & P chain is the largest retail outlet in the world, with 4,400 stores grossing over $5.3 billion a year. A similar degree of concentration exists in frozen foods. There are 250 companies, but Birds Eye (General Foods) and Minute Maid (Coca-Cola) take 20 percent of the business.

While food production becomes more concentrated, retail outlets become fewer. Over 70,000 independent grocers closed shop between 1958 and 1963, along with 2,200 small chains and 2,000 specialty shops. The big food chains claim that within the next decade, there will be fewer than 50 companies selling food.

Food-chain buyers become more powerful each year. And as the small growers' position becomes more desperate, angry charges are heard across the land. A group of Rio Grande tomato growers went to Washington to complain that buyers were forcing them to sell tomatoes at 2 to 4 cents a pound. The same tomatoes were selling in the markets for 39 cents.

When farmers overproduce they teach chain buyers some dangerous tactics. When the poultry farmers flooded the market, chains were urged to buy at any price. They began to use chicken as a loss leader. This drained off the surplus and created a false demand. Production was stimulated nonetheless. Then the chain would stop buying and increase the price of chicken in the store. The housewife, accustomed to low chicken prices, held off buying.

As the surplus piled up, farmers again begged the chains to buy. And so it went, like crack-the-whip.

The price-cost squeeze and the rise of the commercial farm have thus far been to the consumer's advantage. American's eat more and better food for far less money than any people in the world.

But the small farmer has been less fortunate, facing fewer and more powerful buyers. He must either join the march toward vertical integration and go the ignominious way of the poultry farmer, or band together with his fellow farmers. Again, in Van Dyke's words:

"Cannery representatives come around to visit tomato growers one by one. An agent calls on my neighbor, for example, and says, 'Looks like you're in tough this year. They've got more canned tomatoes in the warehouses than they know what to do with. But we've done business together for a long time, so I'll tell you what I'll do. I hate to see you lose out entirely, so I'll give you twenty dollars a ton. Sorry, that's the best I can do.'

"My neighbor says, 'What the heck, fella! You know I'll lose my shirt at that price. I'd be almost as well off just plowing it all under right now.'

"The agent says, 'I know it. But there's nothing I can do. I've got my orders.'

"My neighbor says, 'Well, I'm sure going to have to think this one over. How about coming back day after tomorrow? I want to talk to some of the other guys.'

" 'Better make it tomorrow. We're signing up others right now at twenty dollars. If you wait too long, we'll be signed up for all we can use.'

"My neighbor thinks about the agreement to 'hold the

line at twenty-two fifty.' He looks at his tomatoes in the field, already beginning to show a little pink here and there. He sighs.

"The next day when the agent returns, my neighbor says, 'Look. Can't you make it twenty-one fifty? I hear that's what Heinz is paying.'

"The agent strokes his chin for a minute, and then says, 'Well, we've been friends for a long time. I'll write it up so you'll get bonuses for delivery on Sunday, and what with one thing and another I'll fix it so you'll come out with twenty-one fifty.' "

With his own profits cut to the bone or eliminated altogether, the farmer bears down on his labor costs, the only expense he has that will budge. The farm-machinery and fertilizer companies can set a price and stick to it.

By pushing down on the worker, the small grower avoids the real issue, which is his inferior bargaining position. Many growers feel that the proper time to negotiate is *before planting* instead of *after harvest*.

The canner knows what the market is. He knows if the warehouse is empty or full. Bargaining before planting puts a more nearly equal pressure on both grower and buyer. If a decision is not reached soon it will be too late to plant —something neither wants to see, since they are both hurt if there is no crop. For this to work, the growers would have to present a united front to the buyers—something that has yet to happen.

Unless the present trend is halted, the integrators will take over farming. The real farmer will lose his cherished independence in return for a mediocre job under contract to the canner or packer. Lost in the bargain will be nothing less than our rural civilization.

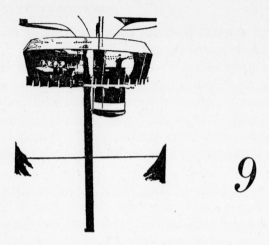

9

O BRAVE NEW FARM

What is the dynamic New Agriculture? It is an agriculture of few but larger, more efficient farms—managed by men highly trained and skilled in the art and technology of agriculture ... It will be energized with the power of risk capital attracted to corporate enterprises by the same basic economy which created and sustains the industrial corporations of America.

—EARL COKE,
vice president of the Bank of America

MECHANIZATION is viewed with mixed feelings by farm workers and unions. It costs them jobs. But automation on the farm, as in the factory, is a fact of life.

Lloyd Fisher, in concluding a thorough study of seasonal farm labor (*The Harvest Labor Market in California*), concluded that "the brightest hope for the welfare of seasonal agricultural workers lies with the elimination of the jobs upon which they now depend . . ."

A farm of the future is on exhibit at the General Motors pavilion at the World's Fair. It is a completely automated farm, without a migrant in sight. Sitting in what looks like an airport control tower, the farmer of the future controls the machines which plant, cultivate, and harvest his crops. The farm is a reclaimed desert and irrigated with converted sea water.

While such a farm is a long way in the future, some crop mechanization is already incredible. The marvels of science have produced mechanical thumbs to test the ripeness of fruit, electronic blueberry pickers, fig harvesters, knockers for almond and olive trees. There are tree shakers for cherries and walnuts, planters for celery, tomatoes, and strawberries, and onion toppers and pickle harvesters. Machines have been developed for harvesting grapes, asparagus, and tobacco. The citrus industry dreams of an electronic vibrator to pick fruit.

Agronomists are busy redesigning the plants to make them more agreeable to machine harvest. A new variety of tomato plant bears simultaneously ripening, thick-skinned tomatoes. A harvesting machine cuts down the whole plant, and the tomatoes are shaken off.

There are hardier sweet potatoes, stringless beans, seedless fruit, and storm-proof cotton.

Far out on Long Island, at Brookhaven National Laboratory, there is a twelve-acre plot of land called the gamma field. Hanging over the center of this field there is a small cylinder. In it is a piece of irradiated cobalt, which is more radioactive than the nation's entire supply of radium. Around this center, fruits, vegetables, plants, and shrubs are planted and exposed to nuclear radiation. The mutations from this weird farm have produced two-headed sunflowers, cancerlike tumors on plants, and silent peanuts (they crumble instead of crunch) for consumption in movie theaters. More useful mutations have brought new varieties of plants with increased yields, and hardier to the adversities of weather and perhaps even to machine handling. Radiation genetics is only beginning.

Machines are already displacing hand pickers in some crops. Over 95 percent of the Massachusetts cranberry crop is now harvested by picking machines.

The Red-headed Okie has made the most dramatic machine triumph. The cotton-picking machine—named for its bright red color—has virtually taken over the cotton fields in many states. A slight increase in picking rates is all it takes to send farmers rushing to buy the machines. In 1962 the Labor Department tried to put a 60-cents-an-hour minimum wage (to prevent "adverse effect") for Mexican braceros used in Arkansas. The then prevailing wage was 40 cents an hour for cotton picking. Six hundred cotton farmers jammed the National Guard Armory in West Memphis to hear Representative E. C. (Took) Gathings lash out at this exorbitant (60-cent) wage. A lone labor leader testified for the increase and was shouted down.

The Labor Department finally backed down to 50 cents an hour. On the strength of this 10-cents-an-hour increase, thousands of Arkansas cotton farmers invested heavily in Red-headed Okies. Today most of Arkansas cotton is machine-picked. The same is true, or soon will be, of most of the cotton states.

Only 6 percent of the nation's cotton crop was mechanized in 1949. Six years later over half had gone to machines. Now in the major cotton states, like California, almost 90 percent is machine-harvested.

Growers, impatient for the machines to rid them of human workers, have turned to animals. Geese are used to weed cotton, and some growers have even tried to teach monkeys to pick fruit.

On Long Island, potato-harvesting machines are taking

over and replacing much of the migrant labor. In 1963 the harvest time in two areas in California was cut from 62,980 man-weeks to 25,600 man-weeks.

So when growers blandly announce that in a few years they won't need farm workers anyway, they are believed. They point to what happened in cotton, implying that the workers must accept the pittance wage or lose his job to one of the marvels of science. "In a few years," said one grower, "there won't be any migrant problems because there won't be any migrants. It'll all be done by machine."

It is easy to overestimate the immediate possibilities of crop mechanization. One of the greatest drawbacks to most harvesting machines is that they are dependent upon the weather. A heavy rain before harvest can make the field muddy, and the machines just won't go.

The cherry-tree shaker, an expensive piece of equipment, has exhibited a tendency to kill the tree roots. The shaker has been tried on peaches and plums without much success. It was used for thinning peaches, but hand-thinning is more thorough and produces a better-quality fruit.

The onion harvester damages the skin, and the market value is considerably reduced.

The apple-tree shaker damages both tree roots and fruit.

For many years to come, mechanization will be difficult or prohibitively expensive in crops "which are particularly soft, which grow irregularly, or which mature at a differential pace so that judgment will have to be left to electronic devices."

According to the Dean of Agriculture at the University of California, the number of workers used is increasing, but in peaks. More workers are needed for shorter times. "Our harvest peaks have not been melting away. History suggests otherwise. Fifty years ago California hired 120,000 farm workers at the peak of the season. Thirty years ago the count had grown to 197,000. By 1950 it had reached 328,000. That's where mechanization set in in earnest. Last year the season's peak toll of farm workers was 370,000.

"So, as our economists look into the future, this is what they see: more mechanization and increased labor productivity; but also growing markets, increased yields from maturing orchards and new cultural methods, *and still more seasonal jobs than we have today.*"

A lengthy study of peak labor requirements of 26 major crops predicts that the labor demands by 1968 will have *increased* in 19 and remained the same in one.

Filling these jobs on the farms of the future may be difficult. As the duration of the jobs decrease, it becomes harder for the individual to make a living.

Little backlashes of consumer revolt may put off the day when the farmer of the future can sit back and watch his computer and his ticker tapes. Mass-farming and mass-merchandising demand a uniformity of quality some consumers are not going to like.

Modern marketing demands that all fresh fruits and vegetables be of machinelike precision: uniform in color, size, and shape so that the housewife won't pick over the selection. It isn't just a sign of old age if you think tomato skins are tougher than they used to be or that the corn isn't quite as tender or the eggs as fresh or the chicken as tasty. In this drive for uniformity, that maxim of the shopping-center culture was never truer: "Plenty of everything. And the best of nothing."

Vegetables in cellophane-wrapped packages can look as if they just came from the field. But they can be two weeks old and taste like wood.

Unless a lot of agricultural experts are wrong, seasonal labor will be an integral part of that brave new farm. When men travel to Mars by rocket, apples will still be picked by hand, by men on ladders.

PART THREE

*Glorious Messenger
Riding Comes*

THE CHURCHES WORKING TOGETHER

MIGRANT MINISTRY

10

THE DO-GOODER

> . . . they are not engaged in agriculture and, therefore, cannot know what they are talking about; they are, at the best, professional do-gooders, theorists, academicians, philanthropists, or dreamers, and at the worst, troublemakers.
>
> —Louisa Shotwell, *The Harvesters*

THE MIGRANT does not live in a totally friendless world. His ally is the "do-gooder," to use the quixotic and condescending term preferred by the growers.

The problems that confront the do-gooder are enormous when he attacks the windmills of migrancy.

In the camps the do-gooder—whether he is a migrant minister, social worker, or concerned citizen—operates in enemy territory. The camps are, after all, on the growers' land. And they usually loathe do-gooders.

The local social worker or migrant minister has his hands

tied. Whatever he does is subject to the arbitrary veto of the grower. Rev. Jack Mansfield, for example, noticed that during the summer heat workers were often sick at the end of the day. A doctor told him they should be taking salt tablets. Rev. Mansfield offered to furnish the tablets if the grower would supervise their daily distribution. (An overdose can be fatal.) The grower refused. He didn't want to be bothered. Another migrant minister filed complaints about the conditions in one camp. Not only did the local authorities refuse to act, but later the minister was barred from the camp.

It is not difficult to see the pattern. The migrant is a temporary necessary evil, as far as the grower and host community are concerned. The local sheriff, the growers, the mayor, the city councilmen, the deacons in the church, the health inspectors, all know each other. For better or worse, they represent the local establishment. They have a common interest in not rocking the boat.

Those sympathetic to the migrants must do their work without seeming to pose a threat to the local power or status quo. Many activities will be viewed benevolently, such as distributing old clothes, holding Sunday school classes for the children in camp, giving free polio vaccine, handing out "health kits" containing such sundry items as toothpaste, soap, and combs. But let them work actively for basic improvements in housing or even mention wages, and the ax soon falls.

If the local health inspector suddenly decides to take his job seriously and starts an active clean-up campaign, he may well find himself among the unemployed, unless the health department is administratively and politically independent—under civil service, for example.

A politician who wants to help the migrants will find the going rough. In assisting people who can't vote, he will arouse the displeasure of people who can. The townspeople who might be sympathetic are generally ignorant of migrant life.

What little they know of the migrants they get from their local newspaper. The average American small-town paper is seldom very probing on sensitive local issues. When the ladies' tea club gives a turkey dinner for the migrants at Thanksgiving, the home-town press writes it up in a big way. Otherwise the arrival and departure of the migrants go unmarked.

A migrant minister in Florida remembered one such occasion. He got a call from a woman who said her club wanted to bring a Christmas dinner out to the camp. He said it was a fine idea. "Now tell me," she said. "What do they like to eat?"

The minister shook his head as he thought about it. "I wanted to tell her these were just people, Americans, and they'd like to have the same kind of Christmas dinner she would. If this was their way of starting some exchange between the town and the camp, I'd have felt better about their charity. But this was it. They wanted to give the migrant a meal and then just turn their backs."

Much of the effort of the do-gooder goes into projects whose scope is necessarily limited. As a cause, the migrant dilemma has never been very popular. While the nation can be periodically shocked by such books as *The Grapes of Wrath*, or more recently by the TV documentary "Harvest of Shame," very little is done. The nation can be roused by the prevalence of physical diseases like polio and tuberculosis, and action will be taken. But the diseases of society, of which migrancy is only one, don't engender the same enthusiasm. As one observer remarked, migrancy can't "happen" to your child.

For whatever reason, do-gooders are scarce among the migrants. The wealthy philanthropists, the generous foundations, have been silent on the subject of seasonal farm labor. And there is only one U. S. senator—Harrison Williams of New Jersey—who can claim an active interest in the problems of migrant labor.

Many people, of course, feel that there is great interest in the migrant worker. The ever-growing pile of articles, reports, and studies on migrant labor is supposedly a sign of this. But close examination of much of the literature on migrancy reveals that its chief object is to whitewash or mitigate. The cheerful faces on the cover, and the glowing text of such reports, hardly present a realistic picture of the misery of migrant life. Much of what sounds like concern for the migrant turns out to be a self-congratulatory tract hailing the great work of a county, state, or civic organization.

And there is that curious backlash of publicity: when much is said about a particular problem, we assume that something has been done or is being done to correct it. This seems to be a phenomenon in the era of mass communication, but Alexis de Tocqueville detected it in 1835 in his appraisal of *Democracy in America*: "As the majority is the only power which it is important to court, all its projects are taken up with the greatest ardour, but no sooner is its attention distracted than all this ardour ceases."

While the terrible conditions of migrancy are occasionally publicized, the effect is often to convince the public that surely something will be done about it. When public attention turns to some other problem, nothing has been changed.

The best work is being done by the American Friends Service Committee, the Migrant Ministry of the National Council of Churches of Christ, and the farm workers "lobby," the National Advisory Committee on Farm Labor, and the Catholic Rural Life Conference.

Under the direction of Bard McAllister, the American Friends Service Committee—the Quakers—operates a kind

of domestic peace corps among the seasonal farm workers in
Tulare County, California.

In the little shoestring communities of Goshen and Tel-
viston, settled by seasonal workers and former migrants,
the Friends were able to organize a town committee. Tel-
viston was an unpopulated tract of wasteland until a
speculator cut it up into lots and sold it to farm workers,
mostly Negroes, looking for a place to settle down. Tel-
viston had no water, no electricity. The town committee
was able to obtain financing to install a $40,000 water
system. Previously water was hauled from the outside.
(The Migrant Ministry is carrying on a similar program
in a fringe Negro community in South Dos Palos.)

The Friends have also started a 170-member farm worker
co-operative to attempt to form a year-round work crew.
The worker co-op has not been a complete success, but in
1963 it paid a 3 percent dividend to the workers.

The oldest of the do-gooders is the Migrant Ministry.
It is over forty years old. On the occasion of this anni-
versary, it gave citations to its earliest leaders, among them
Lila Bell Acheson Wallace, wife of the publisher of the
Reader's Digest, and Josephine Gregory Myers. The work
they started thirty-five years ago is still being carried on
today.

In 1929 Mrs. Wallace established migrant child-care
centers in Riverton, New Jersey, and Houston, Delaware,
for Italian children; and at Bel Air and Preston, Maryland,
for Polish children.

Josephine Myers conducted child-care centers for the
Delaware Italian vegetable workers, who lived in barns
and sheds around the canneries.

Today the Migrant Ministry has ministers in almost
every migrant area. And the support the National Council
of Churches gives legislation favorable to migrants may be
the first time the Protestant churches have openly departed

from the principal of separation between church and state.*

Somewhat restricted by its obligation to the status quo, and to the conservative element within the church itself, the Migrant Ministry has nonetheless been the seasonal farm workers' closest friend.

There is another kind of do-gooder who is less of a friend. Almost every migrant center has some kind of migrant committee. Some are sincere and effective. But there are others that are just for show. The migrant committee will be composed of a group of local citizens headed, in one town, for example, by the wife of the area's largest grower. The function of the committee is to exist. It performs sporadic acts of charity, but its main purpose is to give the impression that "something is being done," and in general to ease the conscience of the local population. (One is reminded of Heywood Broun's description of the man who bought an apple on the street corner and walked away with the air of having solved the entire unemployment problem.)

There are 28 state committees on migratory labor and 28 national organizations dedicated in part or whole to migrant labor. With so much help, it seems that the problems of seasonal farm labor could be solved. But the structure of many of these organizations, notably those on a state level, precludes any real help.

Arkansas set up a state Committee on Migratory Labor in 1959. According to a Labor Department bulletin published in 1960, the committee has supported no legislation, plans no future action, has made no studies, issued no re-

---

* In a pamphlet, *National Goals for the Fifth Decade, 1960–1970*, the Migrant Ministry lists "elimination of foreign farm-labor importation programs," specifically Public Law 78. And: "Justice demands that these employees of the 'factories in the fields' should have the same coverage as other industrial workers by all such legislation as minimum wage, workmen's compensation, child labor laws, and the like."

ports, and has not met.* (The committee did not answer inquiries made in 1964 about its activities.)

The Delaware Committee on Migratory Labor, appointed by the governor in 1957—and given no funds—sent a committee to tour labor camps and make a study of what was being done on behalf of migrants. The committee apparently decided that everything would be all right if only the crew leaders were registered, because the support of such a law is all the future action that was planned.

A member of one state committee on migrant labor described it as "the unfit, appointed by the uninterested, to do the unnecessary."

The South Carolina Committee for the Development and Improvement of Migratory Workers—not improvement of *work conditions*, mind you—supports no legislation, has made no studies, issued no reports, and last met in June of 1958. In the future it plans to amend some laws and improve housing in one county.

The chairman of the Virginia Farm Migratory Committee (in 1960) is a fruit grower. The stated purpose of the committee is to "give advice on and assistance with questions connected with migratory farm labor." It supports no legislation, plans no future action, met once in 1959. No reports. No studies.

State for state, with few exceptions, these committees are interested in only a few aspects of the migrancy within their own states. Nowhere are there any attempts at basic change.

The national committees are more effective. The National Advisory Committee on Farm Labor means business. Headed by Dr. Frank Graham and A. Phillip Randolph, the NACFL tries to keep the public informed about farm labor conditions. They hold public hearings, issue a news-

---

* *State Migratory Labor Committees, Their Organization and Programs*, U. S. Department of Labor, Bulletin 215, 1960.

letter, and follow legislation that will benefit farm workers. It is, in its own words, "a fact-finding, reporting agency." It is both a clearing house of information and a spokesman for the farm workers. (There are other national organizations concerned with migrant labor, and a select list is in the reading notes in the back of the book.)

In discussing the effect of the do-gooders, we necessarily must depart from the sure road of fact and venture onto the uncertain path of speculation.

Excluding the chicken-dinner-once-a-year do-gooder and the do-nothing committee, there is a small but dedicated number of people who is committed to the cause of migrant labor.

Do-gooders alone cannot bring about the basic changes in the migratory labor system that must come. Neither can infrequent outbursts of public indignation or a library full of studies and reports.

But if there were some farm worker organizations or unions who could act in concert with the allies of public opinion and community support, we might see some real progress being made.

11

WILL THE UNIONS MAKE US STRONG?

Farm Workers, we're gaining ground! We're on our way!

—Handbill from the Agricultural Workers
Organizing Committee, AFL-CIO

THE AGRICULTURAL ESTABLISHMENT—the retail food chains, the corporate farms of agribusiness, the labor contractors —all exert pressure on the field worker at the bottom of the heap.

It is a competitive struggle, intense and often vicious, for which the field worker is unprepared.

Efforts to form an agricultural union in America got off to an early and unfortunate start. The Wobblies—the International Workers of the World (called "I Won't Work" by its detractors)—tried to organize farm workers as early as 1905. The Wobblies were a radical, inflammatory group that sprang up in the hobo jungles across the land.

In 1913, the year of the Wheatland Riot, the Wobblies had organized about 8 percent of the migratory labor force. But their power was greater than this would indicate.

The riot on the Durst hop ranch near Wheatland, California, was the first serious outbreak of violence among the migrants. On a hot August morning 2,800 men, women, and children were camped on a hillside, waiting for the harvest to begin.

Durst, according to the custom (then as now), had over-hired. He only needed 1,500 workers. Carey McWilliams, a commissioner of Immigration and Housing in California, described the riot in *Factories in the Field:*

> They came by every conceivable means of trans-portation; many of them had walked from nearby towns and cities. A great number had no blankets and slept on piles of straw thrown on tent floors. The tents, incidentally, were rented from Durst at seventy-five cents a week. Many slept in the fields. One group of 45 men, women, and children slept packed closely together on a single pile of straw. There were nine outdoor toilets for 2,800 people. The stench around the camp was nauseating, with women and children vomiting; dysentery was prevalent to an alarming degree. Between 200 and 300 children worked in the fields; and hundreds of children were seen around the camp "in an unspeakably filthy condition." The workers entered the fields at four o'clock in the morning, and by noon the heat was terrific, remain-ing, as it did, around 105 degrees. The water wells were "absolutely insufficient for the camp" with no means provided of bringing water to the fields. "Nu-

merous instances of sickness and partial prostration among children from 5 to 10 years of age were mentioned . . ." One reason for Durst's chariness about providing water was that his cousin, Jim Durst, had a lemonade concession, selling lemonade to the workers for a nickel a glass. There was no organization for sanitation, no garbage disposal. Local Wheatland stores were forbidden to send delivery wagons to the camp, so that the workers were forced to buy what supplies they could afford from a "concession" store on the ranch . . .

Earnings varied between $1 and 78 cents a day. Over half the workers were destitute and were forced to cash their checks each night. Throughout the season, at least a thousand workers, unable to secure employment, remained idle in the camp.

Two Wobbly organizers got into the camp and called a mass meeting. (Half the workers were aliens from all over the world. Seven translators had to be used.) One of the organizers, Blackie Ford, dramatically held a sick baby up to the crowd and shouted, "It's for the kids we are doing this."

Toward the end of the tense, emotional meeting, the sheriff and his posse arrived and started through the crowd to arrest Ford. A deputy took it upon himself "to sober the crowd" and fired a few shots in the air. That's all it took. The riot started.

When it ended the district attorney—who was also Durst's attorney and had accompanied the sheriff to the meeting—was dead. A deputy was killed along with two workers—a Puerto Rican and an English youth.

The next day the National Guard was called out, and Burns detectives were hired. Wobblies were arrested all over California.

Shur, the other Wobbly organizer at Wheatland, had left

before the riot began. He nonetheless was arrested later in Arizona, shipped back in a boxcar, and "beaten on the average of once a night." He and Ford were tried in Marysville and sentenced to life imprisonment.

But the IWW continued to grow. By 1917, according to Thorstein Veblen, the Wobblies had a union of 50,000. But the same year the Federal Government, alarmed at the revolutionary nature of the IWW, started proceedings against it. Within a remarkably brief time, the Wobblies passed into the limbo of history.

Today in the skid row bars of the farm valley towns, one can still find a few men who can whistle some of the old Wobbly songs. But if you ask them any questions, they just shake their heads and look away.

During the 1930's a series of serious agricultural strikes swept the country. (There were 275 strikes in 28 states, involving more than 175,000 workers. Over half the strikes were in California.) Many of these strikes were led by the Cannery and Agricultural Workers' Industrial Union. Unfortunately, CAWIU (pronounced Ka-Woo) was led by Communists. From 1929 to 1935, CAWIU and the farmer vigilantes slugged it out. Strike leaders were hauled out of jail by masked growers, flogged, clipped, and covered with red paint.

On one occasion during a big cotton strike in the San Joaquin Valley, a group of growers drove up to a union hall and riddled it with bullets. Two workers were killed. Eleven ranchers were arrested and acquitted.

The National Guard was called out during the cotton strike, and the Tulare County fairground was turned into a stockade for strikers. The strike lasted 24 days before it was broken.

By the end of 1934, CAWIU had gone the way of the Wobblies. The state police, the National Guard, the American Legion, and the Associated Farmers vigilantes had stamped out the "unrest."

For the remainder of the nervous thirties, sporadic strikes still broke out despite grower opposition. Once a panicky "strike guard" fired at what he thought was a group of pickets and wounded a golfer on a nearby course.

One of the bitterest strikes was in Hardin County, Ohio. Several hundred onion workers met on a Sunday night in June of 1934 and formed the National Farm Labor Union under the AFL. Most of the workers were from the hills of Kentucky. Some were tenant farmers, some stranded on relief, and some had come off the road. Conditions in Hardin County had deteriorated as the Depression wore on. Onion prices dropped. The soil—a thick black muck— was nearly exhausted and drying up. An onion weeder crawled through it on his knees all day for 12 cents an hour or less.

Families lived in incredible shanties, hungry and poorly clothed. When the strike came, the mountaineers left the fields with grim determination. They had had it.

As National Guard officers and scores of hastily appointed deputies appeared with strike breakers, the trouble started. The union leaders were arrested along with the strikers. Grower vigilante groups formed, and men with rifles stood atop every silo. An onion storage plant was burned, and when strike breakers tried to cross the mountaineers' picket line, riots broke out. Cars were stoned, tires slashed, bombs exploded, and houses burned. When the union leader was released from jail, he was beaten by a mob of strike breakers and dumped in the next county. By September the growers had won. Some of the strikers went back to Kentucky on their own, some were deported, and some waited until spring and went back to the fields.

In 1934 there was a brief strike among migratory workers in New Jersey. State police, along with a group of deputized farmers, quickly settled it in the usual manner.

As the decade ended, the war plants siphoned off much of the surplus labor, and the period of the strikes ended.

Until recently, organized labor has left farm workers to themselves, both in the fields and in the halls of Congress. Most of the social legislation passed in this century has carried farm exclusion as part of the price tag, and labor has bought it, albeit unwillingly.

The AFL-CIO decided in 1959 to try again to organize farm workers, and started the Agricultural Workers Organizing Committee under Norman Smith. In 1961, AWOC led the lettuce strike in the Imperial Valley, and in 1962 started a strike against the California Packing Corporation. Just when AWOC was getting started, the AFL-CIO pulled out the rug by cutting their funds. They have since been restored, but at a considerable cost in membership and morale.

Smith is an old pro at organizing. He learned the business during the organization of the auto industry. He retired in 1964, and plans to live in a labor camp and carry on.

The effect of AWOC is hard to measure. The union claims that conditions in Oregon have improved because growers wanted to keep the unions out. Farm wages in California have risen in the last few years, undoubtedly due in large part to union pressure. AWOC, according to Smith, has spent about $500,000 (as of July 1963) on its organizational drive.

In May of 1961 the Teamsters Union announced that henceforth the field workers at Antle, Inc.—one of the biggest lettuce growers—were members of Local 890. The announcement came as a surprise to everyone, including the workers. It was obviously a "sweetheart" contract, and the courts later threw it out. Rumors continue to circulate that the teamsters are going to go all-out for the field workers.

Other unions, such as the meat cutters' and the packing-house workers', have taken an interest in farm workers. The meat cutters absorbed the National Agricultural Workers Union in 1960.

The task of organizing farm workers is great. AWOC's Henry Anderson has listed the obstacles. Society, he feels, will not support unionization of farm labor for fear of increasing food prices. And there are still many people who are sentimental about the rural "way of life"; they feel unions are out of place here.

The real problems of unionization are the seasonal quality of farming, strong and organized grower opposition, increasing mechanization, and the heterogeneous nature of the farm labor force.*

Furthermore, there is no factory gate in agriculture. The workers are dispersed over large areas. Getting them together is quite a problem. There is no funnel through which the farm workers pass. Unlike the industrial workers, the farm worker *en masse* is inaccessible.

There is also a psychological fact that has to be recognized. Few workers think of themselves as permanently in the farm labor force. Few really believe they will spend their whole life in the field. In fact, it is difficult to find a migrant worker who will tell you he will work the season next year.

Most would leave the field for good if they were able to. Joining a union makes is psychologically "for keeps," and many cannot do this. Although many field workers do not personally object to the work, they are not unaware of the low esteem society places on it and those who do it. As

---

* Field workers and shed workers have little in common. Similar differences exist between the specialized "ladder" workers and the row-crop workers, who do "stoop labor." Ethnic and racial differences are formidable barriers. Also, part-time workers are distinct from interstate migrants, intrastate migrants, and stable seasonal workers.

one migrant said, "I don't mind pickin beans. I just want to know what's wrong with it. Does it mean I ain't human?"

While there is little disagreement over what the problems are, the roads to solution are many. Organized labor—mainly AWOC—has gone one way. The messiahs—to use the unions' contemptuous term—have gone another. The messiah is a worker turned organizer who builds an organization of his own. One such messiah is a young Mexican-American worker in Delano, California.

Cesar Chavez was born in Brawley, California—he has never been to Mexico—and grew up in labor camps and fringe towns of the farm valleys. He attended some forty schools before dropping out in the eighth grade when it became necessary for him to work full-time. "The schools in Brawley were segregated. The Anglos had their schools, and we had ours. I didn't mind this too much. But I always remembered that we got the pencil stubs, the worn-out books."

Fred Ross, a field worker for the Community Service Organization (a community action group), met Cesar in a lumber mill and was impressed by his obvious leadership abilities. He hired Cesar, and the two men toured California on a CSO membership drive.

While he was working with the CSO, Cesar heard reports that workers in Oxnard weren't able to get jobs. He found that growers were using braceros illegally while domestic workers were being turned away.

A growers' association and the Farm Placement Service had a "referral system" going at the time. A worker who applied to the Farm Placement Service office was referred to the growers' association. The growers' association would only hire workers in the carrot fields, where wages were low. The domestic farm workers were unable to get jobs in other crops because of the Mexican nationals, although according to Public Law 78, American workers are to be given preference over the braceros.

For several months Cesar met a group of twenty or thirty workers every morning and went to the Farm Placement Service, got referral cards and applied at the growers' association. And the growers' association would refuse to hire them. Cesar would then return to the CSO office and file a complaint to the director of the California Farm Placement Service. In all, he filed over 1,100 complaints. During this whole time Cesar worked nineteen hours a day, repeating the farcical scene every day with the workers.

During the same time, Cesar went with a group of workers to a field where braceros were working illegally. He telephoned Los Angeles and got an inspector from the Labor Department to come over. When the man got there the grower was told to take the braceros out of the field and hire the local workers. After the labor investigator had left, the local workers were fired and the braceros went back into the fields. This scene was repeated over and over until one day Cesar led a hundred workers back to a field, but not before he had called the newspapers and the television stations. He also called John Carr, head of the Department of Employment, and Edward F. Hayes, head of the California Farm Placement Service.

The march to the field was well covered by the press, and the fact that braceros were working while local workers were unemployed was well documented. After the workers got to the field, Cesar built a small fire, and the workers filed past and burned their referral cards.

As a result of all this, as well as other CSO pressure, a complete investigation was made of the California Farm Placement Service. An assistant chief was fired for taking bribes from growers, Hayes and two other men resigned, and an undisclosed number of employees received "official letters of censure and reprimand." Shortly afterward Hayes became the manager of the Imperial Valley Farmers Association.

Through his experience with the CSO, Cesar learned how to get action. The union he is building, the Farm Workers Association, has members in every valley and camp in California. As of September 1964, there are over a thousand *families* in the FWA.

Cesar draws a salary of $50 a week, which makes him the only known organizer paid by the people he is organizing. The FWA is supported by dues ($3.50 a month), and has no outside help. This is a strong point. "The big union organizers," says Chavez, "come into an area with new cars and a string of credit cards. They spend a lot of money organizing a strike they know ahead of time will fail. And when it does, they move on to a new place. But the worker is left with the consequences. They try to strike and organize at the same time.

"We have a gun with one bullet. We can strike once. But we have to be sure of success. The workers have to strike *and* be prepared to hold out.

"I can walk through any field in the valley and start a strike. It isn't hard. But we want to make it stick. The growers are powerful. And the workers have gotten an attitude of defeat. They're going to lose anyway, so what difference does it make? We're going to show them they can win."

Cesar plans to win, but not by striking. His immediate plans are to offer the growers dependable, well-organized crews made up of Farm Workers Association members. He wants a contract from the grower guaranteeing certain minimums in hours, wages, and working conditions. In return he will sign a "no-strike" contract and provide a stable work force.

It is hard to believe that one man can accomplish more than the best efforts of the AFL-CIO. But it is possible. Most of the members of the Farm Workers Association are Mexican-American. At the beginning of the century the Japanese and Filipinos had crews that worked together and bargained for wages. The common bond of race and a minority status held them together. The same force is working for the FWA. AWOC, on the other hand, must struggle with the formation of a multiracial union in a status-deficient occupation. Cesar's FWA is not segregated. But it has not attracted many Anglos and Negroes.

The chances of a farm-worker union succeeding is not necessarily diminished as the growers become bigger and more consolidated. There is some truth in the contention that the bigger they come the harder to fall.

Photo: Katherine Peake
Deputized growers at a farm labor strike.

12

LULU

Lulu (the heroine of an opera by Wedekind) is an amoral
monster, a sort of Lilith who destroys every man and woman
with whom she comes in contact. She dabbles in murder, per-
version, promiscuity, with equally inhuman indifference. The
point is that society made her that way, and she had no feeling
one way or the other about her actions.

—HAROLD SCHONBERG,
the *New York Times*

THERE IS NO SIMPLE SOLUTION to the "migrant problem."
If an easy solution existed, it would have been discovered
long ago. The ingrained poverty and underemployment
that exists among the seasonal farm workers will be difficult
to eliminate.

Our agricultural system, including the method of harvest,
is the product of a society which, like Lulu, is not only indifferent but destructive and murderous.

It has made harvest work shameful. It has degraded the
very work necessary for its own survival. It has made the
welfare check often more honorable and preferable than
harvest work. It has made pride and satisfaction impossible.
No man goes into a field to harvest crops if there is any
other choice open to him.

If the day ever comes when there is a real labor shortage
in America, when the harvester can walk out of the field
and find a job in town, it won't be easy to lure him back to
harvest. Lulu has made the harvest system akin to slavery.
Free men have to be induced to do unpleasant work.

The stinking camps and the starvation wages will have to
go, along with all the trappings of the old system. Job
prestige is usually more important to a man than salary, but
the prestige of harvesting crops is nil. So salary will have
to make up for it.

In a time of full employment, the wages of harvesting
will soar. This is what the growers have always said they
feared. And their solution has been to throw gasoline on
the fire.

Soaring harvest wages will have the predictable effect of
sending food prices skyward.

Unless Lulu is restrained, unless we stop degrading farm
labor, we will live to regret it. A modernization of the
harvest labor system now will be expensive. But to ignore it
will be to make the price exorbitant.

A special manpower report sent to Congress in 1963
showed that unemployment "represents a loss to the American people of between $30,000,000,000 and $40,000,000,000
a year in loss of additional goods and services."

Louis Krainock, of AWOC, has pointed out that the
American family spends an average of $33 a week on food.
The average agricultural worker (including full-time
workers) spends $22. If this were brought up to average,
it would represent $1,250,000,000 worth of additional food
products a year. And "many of these workers buy cloth-

ing at the Goodwill or surplus store. They don't buy many
new dresses, suits, dress shoes. Just a little increase in their
yearly purchases, say $50 a year, gives you a $100 million
jump in retail trade in clothing alone.

"I won't go down the list of what Americans buy when
they have money. There are autos, TV sets, radios, household appliances, insurance policies and annuities, motor
boats, and recreational equipment, books and baked goods.
The agricultural workers are not buying as they should
because they cannot, and that inability to purchase carries
a price tag of its own."

The low wages in agriculture may seem to be of little
importance to the rest of society. But as the California
Democratic Council has pointed out, "agriculture as a
whole still remains our largest single industry. Depressed
farm purchasing power contributes directly and significantly to fewer sales, fewer jobs, lower business profits,
and a lower general level of national output and income
than what the U.S. economy should be producing."

The marketing of agriculture products needs a thorough
investigation. In many cases neither the grower nor the
worker is getting a fair shake. Tomatoes grown in McAllen,
Texas, and sold in Denver, for instance, produced a net
income (per acre) to the grower of $68.85. But the con-
sumer paid $9,660 for this acre of tomatoes. Only a small
fraction of retail food prices reflect farm crop prices. And
a much smaller fraction represents harvesting wages.

There is room here for fair profits to growers and honest
wages to workers. What the harvesters need is the dignity
of work done under conditions meant for farm workers, not
farm animals.

The issues that are fought over are cabin space, hot water,
and piece rates. But these are only the tangible clothings
of the real issues of basic human rights and fair play.

The migrant doesn't want charity or handouts. He wants
a chance, a start, to build his strength and manage his own
life.

America has never been stronger or wealthier than at this moment. Never has a people been as prosperous as the majority of our citizens. And never has a people lived in such needless poverty as a small part of the underprivileged minority. Never has a people worked harder and suffered more, and got so little for it.

Our material success is unrivaled, yet we have illiteracy, disease, and deprivation of the most primitive kind.

We eat better for less money than any other people. The average American pays 19 percent of his income for food, while the average Russian spends half of his income on his considerably less varied diet.

The wages paid harvest labor constitute a tiny fraction of the retail cost of food. In many cases, an increase in wages of as much as 100 percent would barely affect the retail price. The price to consumer of eliminating migrant poverty is measured in pennies.

Poverty in America, including migrant poverty, can be relieved whenever the people decide it should be. "Never in the history of the United States," wrote Gunnar Myrdal, "has there been a more complete identity between the ideal of social justice and the requirements of economic progress."

During August and September of 1964, Congress extended the first real help to seasonal farm workers. Migratory labor was covered through the President's anti-poverty program. Under the Economic Opportunity Act of 1964, seasonal workers will receive aid in education, child day-care, sanitation, and housing. The amendment to the National Housing Act provides direct loans to profit-making institutions, farm associations, and individuals for the construction of farm-labor housing. Public or non-profit agencies will be given grants or loans.

According to Senator Harrison Williams, Chairman of the Senate Subcommittee on Migratory Labor, the legislative goals for the future are:

(1) an agricultural minimum wage;
(2) collective bargaining rights for farm workers;
(3) prohibition of harmful child labor on the farm;
(4) better recruitment, transportation, and placement procedures for migratory farm workers;
(5) extension and expansion of the Migrant Health Act, currently scheduled to expire on June 30, 1965.

None of the gains made in 1964 represent permanent advances. These are temporary or exploratory measures for the purpose of trying to find an approach to the elimination of poverty in the United States. If these pilot programs are taken as final solutions, we will have wasted the money. Worse, we will have done a grave disservice to the very people we intended to help, by falsely arousing their hopes and by misleading the public into thinking that great strides are being made in the war on poverty.

Laws passed without public sympathy or understanding have seldom succeeded in achieving their goal. And without public support the best desires of government remain lost hopes. Theodore Roosevelt said that "there are things so important that the Government must do them . . ." and he included in this "our object to . . . eliminate as far as possible the conditions which produce the shifting, seasonal, tramp type of labor . . ." and to "prevent the formation of great landed estates . . ."

Each succeeding generation has inherited in ignorance and in silence the forces which have produced these very things. Left in the terrible isolation of his rural ghetto, the migrant American remains a stranger to his country.

For years, the battle for farm labor has been waged in an atmosphere of defeat and despair. There is now a realistic basis for optimism. If there exists any single hope or answer for migrant poverty, it is the same for general poverty, rural and urban. The answer lies, as it should in a democracy, with the people.

READING NOTES

Preface

Every time the income of the migrant is mentioned, the big-farm spokesmen open fire. Their chief complaint is that the $1,000 a year claimed as the average income for farm workers is too low. They maintain that it should include the wages of school children and housewives earning spending money. Migrants, they say, earn "good money."

Migrant income varies considerably across the country. In California, incomes as high as $2,000 are not unusual, while in the East incomes of $500 and $600 are frequently reported.

The growers also insist that actual migrant wages are higher because housing is provided. But it is rare that a migrant gets free housing, and when he does, the value of it can easily be overestimated.

Some growers even imply that the $1,000 a year is really "profit." But the fact is that the migrant handles very little cash. By payday he owes most of it to the crew leader or the store.

While the migrant income has dragged along, the average factory worker earned (in 1963) over $100 a week.

In 1962, the last year for which figures are available, the migrants worked an average total of 116 days and earned—for farm *and* non-farm work—$1,123.

The general condition of farm labor today compares with skilled labor in the nineteenth century. "In *1890* the average pay for unskilled workers was $10 a week and for skilled $20. This did not allow an average family to exist unless the wife and children also

Table 650 MIGRATORY WORKERS WITH 25 DAYS OR MORE OF
FARM WAGE WORK

	Average days worked		Cash wages earned during year	
	At-farm & non-farm wage work	At-farm wage work only	At-farm & non-farm wage work	At-farm wage work only
Year	*Days*	*Days*	*Dollars*	*Dollars*
1949	119	89	594	448
1952	124	87	884	600
1954	156	124	1033	794
1956	143	116	1178	935
1957	131	115	859	745
1959	143	119	911	710
1960	157	123	1016	819
1961	136	109	902	677

SOURCE: *Agricultural Statistics 1962.* Based on data from enumerative sample surveys made by the U. S. Department of Commerce for the Economic Research Service.

worked, as was usually the case. Hours of labor were from ten to twelve each day, six days a week . . . Compensation for death or injury was virtually unknown." (*American History After 1865* by Ray Allen Billington, 1956.)

In the face of these facts, a notion persists that there is money to be made on the season. Growers complain about the high cost of labor, not just as a production expense but according to their concept of what a man "ought" to make. One grower fired a picker who was exceptionally fast and in a good crop was able to earn—on piece rates—around $25 a day. A migrant minister overheard the grower explain that he wasn't going "to pay no nigger no twenty-five dollars a day." The president of a multimillion-dollar grower-packer-shipper citrus farm told me, "Migrants are the scum of the earth. Anything they get over forty cents an hour is gravy."

Some migrants, particularly those new to the game, always figure the next year will be better. "We would have had a good year if we hadn't hit some slack times and bad weather" is a frequent comment. A migrant crew I talked with early in the summer proudly gave their weekly earnings as $90 a week. After a few casual questions, the story came out. They had arrived in camp two weeks before the crop came in. During this time there was no work. Then for a week they worked all day in the fields and all night in the packing sheds. It rained most of the following week, and there was little work. During the week they worked, most of the crew put in sixteen hours a day and made from $80 to $90 a week. (The field work was based on piece rates, and the packing shed used hourly rates. Even those who made $90 that week failed to average $1 an hour.) In other words, the crew had been in camp for one month and had made an average of $20 a week, most of which they owed to the crew leader for room and board. They were leaving for Maryland in the morning for "Red Ripes" and would be a day on the road before they worked again. It is unlikely that they would arrive at the precise moment of harvest. Another week of idleness and further indebtedness to the crew leader would probably pass before the crop was ready.

The meager wages and desperate search for work is only a small part of the migrant story. Once he has found a job, the chances of being killed or maimed on the job are "considerably greater in agriculture than elsewhere." For industry as a whole, a national estimate puts "the number of deaths at 22 per 100,000 workers in 1959. In farming . . . there were 59."* More people are killed in farming than in any other industry. This is particularly appalling when it is remembered that "an estimated 730,000 children (including nonmigrants), 10-18 years of age, were employed in 1959 as paid workers in agriculture."** Only a few states, notably California, have workmen's compensation for domestic farm workers.

The foreign workers are covered (under Public Law 78). The beneficiary of a Mexican bracero is paid $2,000 if he is killed. The bracero is paid $3,000 if he is permanently and totally disabled. The scale works down from $2,000 for the loss of both hands to $50 for the partial loss of one digit.

The Senate once proposed that domestic farm workers be given this same insurance. Only, it offered $1,000 for death and $1,000 for total and permanent disability. The other items for American citizens (feet, hands, eyes) were valued at exactly one-half the corresponding parts for the Mexicans.

The bill was not passed, and domestic farm workers are generally without workmen's compensation, which was the first social insurance given to the *industrial* work force. Maryland passed the first such law in 1902, and by the end of the first World War almost all the states had similar laws.

* *Work Injuries in New York State Agriculture.*
** *The Migratory Farm Labor Problem in the United States.*

And a final comment on the undetermined size of the migrant work force:

In the San Joaquin Valley in California, a huge irrigation system channels the San Joaquin River into a cement canal that runs the length of the valley. The Conservation Service removes the fish ahead of the dam. It's symbolic of our unconcern that we actually care more about the fish in the river than about the migrants in the human stream that harvests the crops of the valley.

1 A Migrant Path Across America

The picture of migrant travel can be found in a potpourri of newspaper clippings, reports, and statistics. Although it is slightly unorthodox for a nonfiction book, the circumstances surrounding the trip of the Beanpicker have been re-created from all these sources. The framework of the trip itself is based on a report by the National Council of Churches. All the names are fictitious, including the name of the bus. (Bus naming is prevalent among the Mexican-American migrants. Louisa Shotwell found these names: The Cold Heart; The Bird Without a Nest; This is Better than Nothing; I Am Going—Who Cares? Who Cares?; and To the Four Winds.)

Some of the case histories in the chapter were taken from two monographs published by the Florida State Board of Health: *They Follow the Sun* and *On the Season*. In the former, Dr. E. L. Koos quoted a police magistrate:

"We don't give them a chance to make trouble. Sure we lock them up quick and fine them more than we would the local people, but we have to—it's the only way to keep them in hand . . . If a local person drove without a taillight, I'd make it ten dollars and costs, or maybe warn them. If a nigger migrant does it, I make it twenty-five and costs. It's the only way we can keep them under control."

Another booklet to which this chapter is indebted is *No Harvest for the Reaper* by Herbert Hill. The reports of the highway accidents appeared in dispatches from the Associated Press and in the Miami *Herald*.

Farm transportation accidents seem likely to remain a prominent feature of migration. In California they have occurred with regularity over the years.

NUMBER OF FARM TRANSPORTATION ACCIDENTS AND NUMBER OF
FATALLY AND NONFATALLY INJURED WORKERS, CALIFORNIA,
1952-1961

		Number of workers injured	
Year	Number of accidents	Fatal	Nonfatal
1952	140	12	304
1953	151	28	341
1954	111	4	161
1955	109	17	158
1956	116	7	344
1957	129	10	377
1958	118	18	357
1959	109	8	329
1960	83	4	130
1961	114	3	174

SOURCE: *Work Injuries in California Agriculture*, 1961, Division of Labor
Statistics and Research, California Department of Industrial Relations.
(Part II of Cobey Committee hearings, Fig. 13, p. 39.)

2   The Crew Leader

The various shake-downs used by many crew leaders are common
knowledge in the trade.

The migrants themselves are fully aware that they are not always
treated fairly, but there isn't much they can do about it. A migrant
worker in North Carolina wrote me that "the average migrant
worker doesn't get the pay he deserves. Why? Because there is
no way of knowing just how much he is supposed to get for the
amount of work he has done. The contractor tells the farmer he
is paying one thing and is paying another. For instance, the contractor tells the farmer that he's paying the worker 15 cents a
bucket for picking tomatoes. He gets the 15 cents and pays the
worker only 12 cents a bucket. That leaves him 3 cents clear on
each bucket of tomatoes that is picked, besides what the farmer is
paying him for hauling the tomatoes and for each picker that he
brings to the field. So you see, a contractor has quite a number of
ways of making money. No wonder he can afford two cars, four
trucks, two buses and have a bank account. We the migrant workers
have made this money for him in order that he can afford these
things." The man who wrote this letter kept books for a crew

leader. He said the crew leader made deductions for Social Security that were never turned in.

In their migrant study in Oregon (*And Migrant Problems Demand Attention*), Current and Infante found thirteen ways the crew leader had of making money:

1) Payment of per capita travel expense by the employing association, with duplicate collection from the migrant.

2) Arrangement for credit for the individual migrant on a percentage fee basis.

3) In handling a contract for an independent farmer, as much as a 50 percent mark-up in housing rental on the farmer's property.

4) Arrangement for tavern credit on a percentage fee basis from the proprietor, who increases prices to pay the fee.

5) Use of the contractor's vehicles in the daily transportation of the workers at about $2.50 per capita weekly.

6) When not hauling workers, rental of vehicles for the hauling of produce.

7) Payment to workers on the basis of as low as $12 per acre instead of the contract price of $13 to $15.

8) In the above instance, deduction of the regular fee from the $12 from each worker.

9) Short-measuring work assignments to the individual worker, netting as much as another $1.50 per day per capita.

10) Payment of fees by crew members ranging from 5 cents to as high as 11 cents per working hour. In co-ordinated operations the crew leader or row boss may retain 2 to 3 cents per hour, with the major share (or about half) going to one of the large contractors. (A few cents an hour may not seem like much, but it becomes significant when one considers, for example, that the four largest Spanish-speaking contractors, who together handled a total of 5,750 workers in western states, received as much as 5,750 times 5 cents for each hour their crews worked (perhaps 30-60 hours per week).

11) Traffic in marijuana.

12) Traffic in prostitution.

13) Collaboration with illegal entries (wetbacks).

The largest contractor they found had his main headquarters in Sunnyside, Washington, and operational headquarters at Madras

(Oregon), Sacramento (California), Payette (Idaho) and Harlingen (Texas).

Approximately 60 percent of the veteran Spanish-American migrants have worked for him at one time or another . . . He has 18 vehicles registered in Oregon, 14 registered in Washington, 6 registered in California, and 4 registered in Texas. His influence among the contractors in Oregon appears to be both feared and envied. He is handling an estimated 2,200 hands this year in the state of Oregon, and operates through some 22 subcontractors or crew leaders. The estimate of those who know his operation, whether reliable or not, is interesting—$800 a day clear.

A contractor of equal or nearly equal influence carries with him a group of skillful gamblers. He himself is regarded as an expert gambler and he makes no effort to hide this . . . He is an excellent talker and his favorite subject is "proper housing for migrants."

An Anglo-American contractor was one of the most colorful people we met in the migrant labor world. His base of operations is in Arizona and some of his crew are southern Negroes. He has a beautiful way of confusing an investigation. For example, when he thinks he may be observed, he drives an old car. However, when we finally found his main camp, we found his 40-foot house trailer and his 1958 (then new) Chrysler Imperial automobile. He dresses his part constantly and we never encountered him dressed in anything but a dirty shirt and dirty trousers, and with unclean beard stubble.

The best argument yet summoned by the apologists for the crew leaders is that they aren't all bad. This is, of course, beside the point. The real point is that the crew leader can be dishonest and get away with it.

There is a lot of double-talk about crew leaders. Expressed in the official language of the Employment Security Commission, the crew leader is explained thus:

Lack of sufficient experienced supervisors was another source of misunderstandings and tended to impede improvement of employer-employee relations. Most crew leaders lacked sufficient elementary education to absorb education relative to good psychological practices used by successful supervisors. It was apparent that these crew leaders used "might" in lieu of

DOMESTIC AGRICULTURAL MIGRANTS IN THE UNITED STATES

COUNTIES ESTIMATED TO HAVE 100 OR MORE AT PEAK OF A NORMAL CROP SEASON

943 COUNTIES

	100 - 500
	500 - 3,000
	3,000 - 10,000
	10,000 or more

Public Health Service Publication No. 540
(Revised 1960)

good supervisory techniques and methods. Such action failed
to win acceptance by many workers.*

3 The Tar-Paper Curtain

Migrant housing is another favorite subject for reports, and there
are hundreds of them. The cabin is a tangible sign of migrant
poverty. To provide a vehicle for existing research and my own, I
have used "Shacktown,"** a composite camp which comes as close
to an "average" migrant camp as I can imagine. The description
of the camp that was the destination for Little Jim's crew is based
partly on a camp I visited in Springdale, Arkansas. Some of the
more valuable reports used to describe Shacktown were:

*A Preliminary Report on the Study of Farm Laborers in Fresno
County* by Beatty, Pickford, and Brigham (A Rosenberg Foundation Project).

Housing for Florida's Migrants is a report prepared for the
President's Commission on Migratory Labor by the U.S. Department
of Labor and the Florida Industrial Commission.

Migrant Project 1959 was made in Palm Beach County, Florida,
by the State Board of Health.

Strangers in Our Fields by Ernesto Galarza is a booklet sponsored
by the Fund for the Republic, which describes the condition of
Mexican field workers.

A Cuban-born Miami lawyer, Albert Rosillo, wrote an article
for the Miami *Herald* (March 15, 1957) on his experience in a
labor camp. Parts of this article were incorporated in the description of Shacktown.

Some of the comments of the Shacktown residents came from
the *Farm Labor Experience Survey*, prepared in 1959 by the
Migrant Ministry from interviews with two hundred farm families.

In 1960, when CBS presented "Harvest of Shame," the citizens
of southern Florida felt they had been betrayed. The Palm Beach
Post, on February 8, 1961, issued a special newspaper supplement
to give the "Glades Side of the Story." They made some points.
Edward R. Murrow *had* made some mistakes. He had said that no

---

* *Farm Labor Report, Post Season 1962*, Michigan Farm Placement
Service, Employment Security Commission, 1963.

** After this was written I discovered a fringe community in Florida
actually called Shacktown.

migrant's child had ever been to college. They found some who had.

The Belle Glade chief of police had stated, on the CBS program, that "they [the migrants] sleep around the bars and on the grass and in the packing houses around the lake area, in the parks. Any place they can find to sleep and rest for a few hours." But, protested the *Post,* the police chief had meant that that was the way things were thirteen years ago, when he took office. "But the film made it appear that the condition still prevails," the chief said in the *Post* interview. "Actually it doesn't."

The year before, a public health team from Palm Beach's own Health Department reported in *Migrant Project 1959* that "an estimated 20,000 workers, excluding other household members, return to the 'Glades' area of Palm Beach County between October 15 and November 15. At the beginning of the season, a wide choice of housing is available. *Within the next 30 days, the acute housing shortage becomes apparent when families are discovered living in condemned housing, cars, old bus bodies, and hastily constructed lean-tos on canal banks and in cane breaks"* [italics added]."

The testimony on field sanitation was taken from the hearings before the Subcommittee on Migratory Labor of the Committee on Labor and Public Welfare of the U.S. Senate. The hearings were held during July and August of 1962. The bill under consideration was to "provide sanitation facilities for migratory farm workers." Parts of the bill have been included in the President's anti-poverty legislation.

4 The Children of Harvest

The most tragic part of migrancy is the damage to the child. Almost everything ever written on farm labor mentions child labor. The whole bibliography is a general substantiation of this chapter.

One of the more factual reports was made to Governor Edmund G. Brown of California by the state director of Public Health, Dr. Malcolm H. Merrill: *Health Conditions and Services for Domestic Seasonal Agricultural Workers and their Families in California.* It is interesting to note that it was released on October 1, 1960, although the primitive life it reveals sounds more like the darker days of the Depression.

Migrant Project 1959 has already been cited.

The song "Calling for Migrants" was found in a packet of informational material from the National Council of Churches. The arithmetic problem is from *Knowing and Teaching the Migrant*

Child by Elizabeth Sutton. In addition to the sociological arithmetic problem, there was a story written for sixth-grade readers, a sugar-coated tale called "Lucy Picks Beans":

"Lucy was so excited she could scarcely sleep. Every hour or two she jumped out of bed to peep at the clock ticking noisily on the shelf. What little sleep she got was filled with dreams of the trip on the truck to the bean field . . ." And so on. Lucy just couldn't wait. Compare this with an essay actually written by Isaac, an eight-year-old migrant child in an experimental school in Potter County, Pennsylvania. (The school was run by the National Child Labor Committee and the Pennsylvania State University.)

"Get down on your knees. Then start picking beans. When you get two hampers full, then you weigh them. After you weigh them, you put them on the truck. But before you put the beans on the truck you put them in a sack. You must pick beans all day. You go home when the man tells you."

The comments of the Texas doctor were taken from a public hearing of the National Advisory Committee on Farm Labor, held in Washington in 1959. A summary of the hearing was published in a booklet, *Report on Farm Labor,* in New York.

The little girl killed by the potato-digging machine was described in a *Good Housekeeping* magazine article on child labor by A. E. Farrell (November 1960).

The story of the girl who fell asleep in the pile of burlap bags was told to me by Cesar Chavez.

The difficulties of educating migrant children are often compounded by resistance within the family. The following case histories from *Working with Migrant Children in Our Schools,* a mimeographed report from Florida, emphasize this. And they further describe a bleak childhood.

The Johnson family is composed of seven people. They were housed in a trailer in a substandard housing unit on the outskirts of Belle Glade for two months, in October and November of 1956 . . .

A freeze had halted work in the cabbage field where the parents had worked, and the family was living on cabbage, grapefruit which had been given to them, and fish which they caught, mostly at night. The teacher was easily able to understand why Mary could not eat fish or cabbage when it appeared on her plate in the cafeteria . . .

The mother said that the only time the family had done well in the past year was when all the family members worked in the field. The Johnson family was in South Bay three weeks before they left for the strawberry area in Florida. The children came for their report cards before they left. Mary quoted her mother as saying that they would not have to go to school there.

The Parker family, composed of nine people with three school-age children, came to the Glades area for the first time this year. They lived in a tin shelter at Osceola Center for six weeks and the children attended Osceola School . . . The children began to show much progress in school. They asked to take their books home so they could read to their mother . . . One day they were absent, and the attendance worker went to the home to inquire about them. The mother told her that they were sick, and the father had taken them to the doctor. Later in the day the attendance worker found them in a bean field. The father was furious when he found they would have to go to school. A week later the family left the community, leaving no information about their destination.

5 Farewell to Gothic America

The statistics on production are from an article in the *New York Times Magazine*, June 2, 1963. The article, "Now the Non-Farmer Asks for Parity," is by Edward Higbee, a professor of land utilization at the University of Rhode Island. He is one of the sharpest critics of "organized agriculture." Professor Higbee asserts that agribusiness, mainly through the American Farm Bureau Federation, is "maneuvering to keep its grip on the taxpayer's wallet."

The taxpayer is led to believe that American agriculture is in a financial plight, but this is only because the incomes of small part-time and semiretired operators have been averaged in with the professionals. "If children's lemonade stands were included in a census of retail establishments in the same manner, even the A&P could be shown to qualify for government aid."

I found the report of the North Carolina Land Commission in the university library at Chapel Hill. It seemed to voice an appeal which evidently was ignored at the time and still is.

6 It All Started with Columbus

Most of the material for this chapter is from Edward Higbee's *Farms and Farmers in an Urban Age*; Carey McWilliams' *Factories in the Field* and *Ill Fares the Land; Fields of Bondage* by Henry P. Anderson; and *Farmers in a Changing World, the 1940 Yearbook of Agriculture.*

I am also indebted to a master's thesis by R. H. Campbell, *A Study of Negro Migrant Agricultural Workers in a Long Island Camp,* and an article in the Miami *Herald* (February 28, 1960) by Nixon Smiley, the farm editor. The research papers of AWOC were consulted for statistics.

The transcript of the Cobey Commission Report (already cited) has a brief, well-documented history of the development of California agriculture.

Wilma Dykeman and James Stokely have written about the development (or fall) of southern agriculture with great insight and passion in *Seeds of Southern Change.* (His family owns the Stokely-Van Camp grower-packer-shipper company, but he has no part in the company, preferring, as he puts it, "to grow and can ideas.")

A ditty well known to most southerners ran:

> You can't make a livin'
> On sandy lan';
> I'd druther be a nigger
> Than a po' white man.

The land—the black man—the poor white: held together by unbreakable bonds of mutual need, separated by generations of misuse and uncertainty and mutual fear. The Great Depression hit the rest of the country after a period of boom prosperity, but in the rural South it merely intensified an economic crisis that had plagued the region for years. Its roots ran deep into the past, into the very founding of the plantation economy.

There were four basic elements required for a successful plantation system. Rupert Vance listed them in 1929: first, land—extensive fertile level or rolling acres; second, labor—unskilled, plentiful, docile, and cheap; third, management—to maintain a social as well as economic supervision of the labor supply; and fourth, crop—a routine, easily marketable cash staple.

At the end of the Civil War, the South, its people, and especially its cotton plantations were destitute. The planter had his land but no money for taxes or seed or financing for a crop. The black man who had been a slave now had freedom, a freedom which meant mobility but not security; and without the forty acres and a mule of which he had dreamed, he possessed neither land nor tangible capital but only the muscle and sweat which had been his traditional contribution to the ante bellum agriculture. The small white landowner had a little land and his own labor—insufficient acres to secure loans for capital and no tradition of paternalism to assist him in personal crisis. Between the upper rail and the mud sill, he was caught in a squeeze—never "as good" as the gentry, always "superior" to the Negro, he helped keep each in his place. From what has been called this "network of dependencies" the cropper plantation arose.

The planter put his land up for security and scraped together enough money to finance next year's crop. The black man put up his labor, and the planter "furnished" him seed and livestock and home and food to carry him through the year until the harvest, when he received his share of the crop, usually one-half, in return for his labor. Thus sharecropping was born—an expedience that became a way of life, defined a system whereby labor was secured without wages, and loans were made without security. Both the planter and the cropper might have agreed with the ironic humor of Louis XIV when he said, "Credit supports agriculture as the cord supports the hanged."

7 Strangers in Our Fields

The two men who probably know most about the use and misuse of braceros are Henry Anderson and Ernesto Galarza. Both have written well-documented books on the subject: *Strangers in Our Fields* (Galarza) and *Fields of Bondage* (Anderson). The material about the Reception Center is from the latter book.

This incident is not an isolated example. There are hundreds of other stories very much like it. One of the "ideal" features about all the labor import programs is that any worker who has a complaint can be sent home quietly. A Long Island farmer was quoted in the National Advisory Committee's *Report on Farm Labor* (already cited):

"O no, I want BWI's [British West Indians]. When I get ahold of their permits, they gotta stay put and they know it. If they make a move, they'll be thrown outta the country. They don't make any trouble!"

The accountant for the El Centro lettuce company, Elizabeth Longenbohn, issued a six-page notarized statement on her falsification of the payroll records of the R. T. Englund Company. The statement was made available to me by Mrs. Katy Peake of the Emergency Committee to Aid Farm Workers in Los Angeles.

The letter by Rafael, "To Anyone Who Cares," was reprinted from the March 1959 *Packinghouse Worker*, published in Los Angeles.

An additional note is necessary on Fred Van Dyke's charge that growers and contractors made huge profits feeding braceros.

John Zuckerman, a San Joaquin grower, and past member and president of various California growers' associations, denied that it was possible to profit substantially from feeding the braceros. He claimed that after all costs are deducted there is only a small profit.

The charge, however, is supported by the Emergency Committee to Aid Farm Workers. This committee includes the familiar names of Steve Allen, Eugene Burdick, Carl Sandburg, John Steinbeck, Dore Schary, and Robert Ryan. In a "Statement of Conscience" the committee made the following charges:

> Immense profits have been made from furnishing meals to braceros "at cost." This is the primary reason labor contractors—the same labor contractors who are supposed to be "excluded" from the program—fight among themselves for the privilege of feeding braceros, pay kickbacks to association managers, and wine and dine officials. A contractor near Tracy, California, made over a quarter of a million dollars from the "nonprofit" feeding of braceros in the space of a few years. The manager of a bracero camp in Santa Barbara has developed an ingenious improvement over the techniques of garden-variety operators. He has set up a catering firm which provides meals in his camp. He is president of the catering firm. And he has established a wholesale grocery firm which sells foodstuffs to the catering firm. He makes his profits three ways.

With the expiration of the bracero program—Public Law 78—a new chapter begins in the history of harvest labor. Some observers, like economist Eric Thor, have predicted a new wave of Okies from the southern states. They will flock to the West to take over the jobs vacated by the braceros. Thor contends that the new Okies will flood California and the relief rolls. But there still won't be enough workers to handle the brief seasonal peaks.

In other words, too many and then too few.

The *New York Times* reported on February 22, 1964 that earlier in the year John V. Newman, a "prominent Ventura citrus grower and first president of the Council of California Growers, announced the decision of California agriculture to accept abandonment of the bracero program as a 'fact of life' . . . Mr. Newman won the support of the State Board of Agriculture in a proposal to Governor Edmund G. Brown to throw California's resources behind a campaign to develop a new labor supply. It was estimated that 40,000 new farm labor families would be needed to replace the braceros." This must be bitter-sweet irony to the workers who have tried to get jobs in years past.

Labor contends that California has plenty of farm workers now.

ESTIMATE OF TOTAL NUMBER OF HIRED FARM WORKERS BY RECORD OF SOCIAL SECURITY ACCOUNTS FOR CALIFORNIA—1962*

Individuals who worked temporarily and year-round in agriculture at some time during the third quarter of 1962 as determined by employer reports of S. S. Accounts (from California Department of Employment unpublished report, May 1963) 362,799

Individuals who worked during the other three quarters of 1962 but not the third quarter, or were not identified by employers. *Estimate* 45,000

TOTAL HIRED DOMESTIC FARM WORKERS 407,799

1962 peak number of hired domestic farm workers—Sept. 1962 (from California Department of Employment, Report 881 M#1, Jan. 1963) 258,000

EXCESS OF TOTAL HIRED DOMESTIC FARM WORKERS OVER PEAK

NUMBER 149,799

* Newsletter of the Emergency Committee to Aid Farm Workers, Inc., July 1963.

8 *The Integrators*

Concern over the chains' buying power is finally taking shape. In a recent address to Congress, President Johnson said:

"The recent changes in the marketing structure for distribution of food are as revolutionary as those in production. There are some 200,000 retail grocery stores, but we know that $1 out of every $2 spent for groceries goes to fewer than 100 corporate, voluntary, or co-operative chains. Our information about how this greatly increased concentration of power is affecting farmers, handler, and consumers is inadequate. The implications of other changes that take place as vertical integration and contract farming have not been fully explored. I urge a bipartisan commission to study and appraise these changes."

Commenting on the speech, the *New York Times* said editorially: "An investigation may actually serve to erase the widely held notion that both farmers and consumers are being cheated by food profiteers."

A recent report confirms the notion ("Low Man on the Totem Pole," issued by the Denver Union Stockyard Company). It concluded that "food chains are exercising their power in an increasingly irresponsible manner which has the effect of controlling, manipulating, or administering both producer and consumer prices."

9 *O Brave New Farm*

Seasonal Labor in California Agriculture, a 200-page mimeographed book by the Division of Agricultural Sciences of the University of California, gives a good analysis of anticipated farm labor demands.

The *Farm Labor Report, Post Season 1962* of the Michigan Employment Security Commission contains a good run-down on mechanization in that state.

The description of radiation genetics is from the September 1963 issue of THINK magazine (IBM). The article, "Radiation Is Producing Better Vegetables," is by Harland Manchester.

Science on the farm has not been confined to harvest. Purdue University scientists are experimenting with "climate control" for chickens, turkeys, pigs, and beef cattle. And according to the *New York Times* (September 28, 1963), there is talk about air-conditioned buildings for animals in the future. "Similarly, farm engineers have taken hogs out of the mud and put them in insulated housing." Migrant workers have long complained that their camps are not fit for pigs, which apparently is true.

10 *The Do-Gooders*

The Labor Department booklets, *State Migratory Labor Committees*, Bulletin 215, and *National Organizations for Migrant Farm Workers and Their Families*, Bulletin 236, list the groups interested in farm labor. In the "Reading Notes" on Chapter 12, I have listed the organizations which I personally feel are most important.

11 Will The Unions Make Us Strong?

The Emergency Committee has compiled a list of the major
strike activities in the West, which is to say, in the country.

(a) DiGiorgio Fruit Corporation, Arvin, California, 1947–
1949. The National Farm Labor Union (later National
Agricultural Workers Union) sought union recognition.
Government officials openly escorted braceros through the
union's picket lines. As one of them later said, "After all,
it was our job to see that the nationals got work." Union
leaders considered the use of braceros, particularly for
critical skilled tasks, such as irrigation, decisive in the
breaking of the strike.

(b) San Joaquin and Stanislaus counties, California, September–
October, 1950. Some 2,000 braceros, "escorted" by highway patrolmen and private police, worked behind picket
lines and broke a strike of 3,500 domestic tomato workers.

(c) Imperial Valley, California, April 1951. The NFLU organized domestic cantaloupe workers around demands of
union recognition, wage increases, and removal of wetbacks from the area. Union members themselves were
largely successful in removing wetbacks, but found to
their dismay that wetbacks were promptly replaced by
braceros, escorted through picket lines, as usual, by armed
guards.

(d) Imperial Valley, May–June, 1952. Domestic cantaloupe
pickers struck against wage slashes. The strike was virtually
100 percent effective among domestic workers. Throughout the entire remainder of the season, the Department of
Labor pondered the question of whether a labor dispute
existed, during which time the Imperial Valley Farmers
Association was authorized to bring in the cantaloupe crop
with braceros working under the slashed wage scale.

(e) Between 1954 and 1959, the National Agricultural Workers Union found its members replaced by braceros when
it attempted collective action in Monterey County carrots,
San Joaquin County asparagus and tomatoes, Sutter
County peaches, Fresno County cantaloupes, and other
crop areas.

(f) During the same period, United Packinghouse Workers of
America, AFL-CIO, Local 78, has conducted perhaps ten

or twelve strikes in California. These strikes have involved lettuce, carrot, celery, melon, and other operations
formerly performed in packing sheds but now moved into
the fields, where they are performed by braceros at approximately half the former wages. Virtually every one
of UPWA's strikes has been broken by the unrestricted
use of braceros behind the union's picket lines. A recent
instance took place in strawberries in the Salinas Valley,
May 1961.

(g) Braceros worked behind picket lines of the Agricultural
Workers Organizing Committee, AFL-CIO, during September 1960, at the tomato plantations of the Cochran
Company, San Joaquin County, California. The Department of Labor gave its consent to this proceeding, and the
strike was effectively broken.

(h) Braceros worked behind AWOC picket lines at the Bowers
peach ranch, Butte County, California, during August 1960.

(i) Imperial Valley lettuce harvest, January–March, 1961. For
nearly two months, AWOC, UPWA, and the Government of Mexico insisted that the Department of Labor
enforce the law, and remove braceros from the struck
area. It did not do so. The lettuce harvest was completed
by braceros, and the strike was broken.

It is regrettable that agricultural employers have been so be-
dazzled by the lure of captive labor, deposited at their gates
by an agency of government, that they are blinded to the fact
that stabilization of a labor market always works to the ultimate
advantage not only of workers but employers as well.*

At the hearings of the National Advisory Committee in Washington, February 5, 1959, George Smith, a sharecropper, migrant,
and union organizer, testified about his attempts to help organize
the sugar-cane workers:

In 1953 I was called down to Louisiana to help in an organizing campaign. We signed up about 2,000 sugar cane
plantation workers on some of the big plantations. The sugar-
mill and refinery workers were already organized, so the
plantation workers wanted to be organized. We tried to get
the sugar corporations to bargain with us. They refused to do
so. There was a strike of sugar-cane workers. It wasn't for

* "Statement of Conscience and a Review of Evidence" by the Emergency Committee to Aid Farm Workers, March 29, 1963.

wages but just for the right to organize. After six weeks the strike was broken by court injunctions. The Louisiana courts said it was a conspiracy for farm workers to get together and act in concert during the harvest season. The sugar cane plantation workers' case was appealed to the United States Supreme Court. A few of my friends who didn't have any money signed papers saying they were paupers so it wouldn't cost anything to get up to the highest court. The union didn't have any money to pay the costs. The AFL and the CIO, then separate organizations, both turned us down. Some lawyers here in Washington, Mr. Joe Rauh and Mr. Dan Pollitt, took our case into the Supreme Court and didn't charge us any fees either. Nearly two years after the strike was broken up, the Supreme Court held that the Louisiana courts were wrong and that they should not have stopped the sugar workers from joining a union and striking. The union won its point, but the workers lost. I have been in and out of Louisiana since, helping some of the sugar-mill workers, and I saw a lot of our old-time members on the plantations. Their wages are still low, 40 to 50 cents an hour. They want a union but they are afraid to start again all by themselves. I guess they are just waiting for the AFL-CIO that promised to organize the unorganized about four years ago, to get around to helping them, too.

The day after George Smith spoke, James B. Carey, vice president of the AFL-CIO, said, "I think the labor movement has finished with procrastination, has had done with evasion.

"American unionism, I believe, is going to put this issue of farm labor and sharecropping high—very high—on its priority list of things to be done."

Three years later, the AFL-CIO cut off the funds for AWOC.

12 Lulu

Those readers interested in learning more about migrants should write the following organizations for further information:

American Friends Service Committee
Community Relations Division
160 North 15th Street
Philadelphia 2, Pennsylvania

Mr. R. P. Sanchez, Chairman
Committee on Migratory Labor
American GI Forum of the U. S.
223 South 17th Street
McAllen, Texas

The Very Rev. Msgr. William J. Quinn
Executive Secretary
Bishops' Committee for Migrant Workers
1300 South Wabash Avenue
Chicago 5, Illinois

The Rev. John A. Wagner, Executive Secretary
Bishops' Committee for the Spanish-Speaking
828 Fredericksburg Road
San Antonio 1, Texas

Mr. Louis Zarate, National President
Community Service Organizations, Inc.
2701½ East 4th Street
Los Angeles 33, California

Miss Fay Bennett, Executive Secretary
National Advisory Committee on Farm Labor
113 East 19th Street
New York 3, New York

Mr. Herbert Hill, Labor Secretary
National Association for the Advancement of Colored People
20 West 40th Street
New York 18, New York

The Rev. Edward W. O'Rourke
Executive Director
National Catholic Rural Life Conference
3801 Grand Avenue
Des Moines 12, Iowa

Miss Elizabeth B. Herring, Executive Secretary
National Council on Agricultural Life and Labor
1751 N Street, NW
Washington 6, D. C.

The Rev. E. Russell Carter
Director of Migrant Work
Division of Home Missions
National Council of Churches
475 Riverside Drive
New York 27, New York

Miss Helen Raebeck, Director of Public Affairs
National Council of Jewish Women
One West 47th Street
New York 26, New York

Senator Harrison A. Williams, or
Mr. Frederick R. Blackwell, Counsel
Subcommittee on Migratory Labor
Senate Office Building
Washington 25, D. C.

Miss Vera Rony, National Secretary
Workers Defense League
112 East 19th Street
New York 3, New York

Any of these organizations will keep you informed of migrant conditions and pending legislation that will affect the farm workers.

BIBLIOGRAPHY

Books, monographs, pamphlets, booklets, etc.

Agee, James, *Let Us Now Praise Famous Men.* Boston: Houghton Mifflin Company, 1939.

Agribusiness and Its Workers. National Advisory Committee on Farm Labor, New York, 1963.

Agricultural Employment in Arizona, 1950–1962. Arizona State Employment Service, Phoenix, 1963.

Agriculture, CDC Issue Program 1963. California Democratic Council, Bakersfield, 1963.

Anderson, Henry, *Fields of Bondage.* Mimeographed, 1963.

———, *To Build a Union.* Mimeographed, 1963.

Arizona Cotton Production Survey. Arizona State Employment Service, Phoenix, 1961.

Arizona Lettuce Production Survey, 1961–62. Arizona State Employment Service, Phoenix, 1963.

Beatty, William C., Jr., Pickford, Patricia, and Brigham, Thomas M., (of the Fresno County Rural Health and Education Committee), *Preliminary Report on a Study of Farm Laborers in Fresno County from January 1, 1959 to July 1, 1959.*

Beck, James W., *Hired Labor Survey.* Grand Forks: University of North Dakota, March 1958.

A Better Life for Farm Families. National Sharecroppers Fund, New York, 1963.

The Blight on the Countryside. National Agricultural Workers Union, Washington, 1959.

Browning, R. H., and Northcutt, T. J., Jr., *On the Season*. Florida State Board of Health, Jacksonville, 1961.

Bureau of Migrant Labor Report. New Jersey Department of Labor and Industry, Trenton, 1961.

California's Farm Labor Problems, Parts I & II (mimeographed). The Cobey Committee, Senate of the State of California, Division of Agricultural Sciences, Sacramento, 1961 and 1963.

California Farm Reporter (monthly bulletins, 1963 and 1964). 740 Hilmar Street, Santa Clara, California.

Campbell, R. H., *A Study of Negro Migrant Agricultural Workers in a Long Island Camp*. Unpublished thesis, undated.

Capps, Betty, *A Survey of the Migratory Family Unit Farm Labor in Springdale, Arkansas*. Unpublished thesis, undated.

Current, Tom, and Infante, Dr. Mark Martinez, *And Migrant Problems Demand Attention*. Bureau of Labor, Salem, Oregon, 1959.

Dykeman, Wilma, and Stokely, James, *Neither Black Nor White*. New York: Rinehart, 1957.

————, *Seeds of Southern Change*. Chicago: University of Chicago Press, 1962.

The Farm Labor Policy of the Federal Government. National Council on Agricultural Life and Labor, Washington, 1960.

Farm Labor Report, Post Season 1962. Michigan Farm Placement Service, Employment Security Division, Detroit, 1963.

Fisher, Lloyd H., *The Harvest Labor Market in California*. Cambridge: Harvard University Press, 1953.

Galarza, Ernesto, *Strangers in Our Fields*. Joint United States-Mexico Trade Union Committee, Washington, 1956.

Galbraith, John Kenneth, *The Affluent Society*. Boston: Houghton Mifflin Company, 1958.

Hardman, R. L., *No Other Harvest*. New York: Doubleday & Company, 1962.

Harrington, Michael, *The Other America*. New York: The Macmillan Company, 1963.

Higbee, Edward, *Farms and Farmers in an Urban Age*. New York: The Twentieth Century Fund, 1963.

Higbee, Edward. Governor's Conference with . . . The Governor's Office, Raleigh, N. C. 1964.

Hill, Herbert, *No Harvest for the Reaper*. The National Association for the Advancement of Colored People, New York, 1959.

Koos, E. L., *They Follow the Sun*. Florida State Board of Health, Jacksonville, 1957.

Learning on the Move. Colorado State Department of Education, Denver, 1960.

Manis, Jerome G., *A Study of Migrant Education.* Kalamazoo: Western Michigan University, 1958.

McWilliams, Carey, *Ill Fares the Land.* Boston: Little, Brown & Company, 1942.

———, *Factories in the Field.* Boston: Little, Brown & Company, 1939.

Merrill, Malcolm H., M.D., *Health Conditions and Services for Domestic Seasonal Agricultural Workers and Their Families in California.* California State Department of Public Health, Sacramento, 1960.

Migrant Project 1959. Florida State Board of Health and the Palm Beach County Health Department, Jacksonville, July 1959.

Migratory Farm Workers in the Atlantic Coast Stream (Changes in New York, 1953 and 1957). Cornell Agricultural Experiment Station, Ithaca, 1960.

Myers, Robin, *The Position of Farm Workers in Federal and State Legislation.* The National Advisory Committee on Farm Labor, New York, 1960.

Myrdal, Gunnar, *A Challenge to Affluence.* New York: Pantheon Books, 1963.

National Goals for the Fifth Decade, 1960–1970. National Council of Churches, New York, 1961.

New Mexico Farm Placement Program. New Mexico Employment Security Commission, Albuquerque, 1960.

Peterson, William H., *The Great Farm Problem.* Chicago: Henry Regnery Company, 1959.

Providing Education for Migrant Children. Colorado State Department of Education, Denver, 1961.

Religion and Labor. Bulletin of the Religion and Labor Council of America, Columbus, Ohio. May 1959.

Report on Farm Labor. National Advisory Committee on Farm Labor, New York, 1959.

Seasonal Labor in California Agriculture. Mimeographed, University of California, Berkeley, 1962.

Shotwell, Louisa R., *The Harvesters.* New York: Doubleday & Company, 1961.

———, *This is the Migrant.* New York: Friendship Press, 1958.

Statement of California Labor Federation. AFL-CIO, before the Agricultural Labor Commission, San Francisco, 1962.

Statement of Conscience and a Review of Evidence. The Emergency Committee to Aid Farm Workers. Mimeographed, March 29, 1963.

Steinbeck, John, *The Grapes of Wrath.* New York: Harper & Brothers, 1939.

Survey of Effects of the Mechanical Bean Harvester in New York State, 1958. New York State Department of Labor, New York, 1959.

Sutton, Elizabeth, *Knowing and Teaching the Migrant Child.* Department of Rural Education and the National Council on Agricultural Life and Labor Research Fund, Washington, 1962.

Teaching Children Who Move with the Crops. Fresno County Project, Fresno County Department of Education, Fresno, California, 1955.

Third Annual Conference on Families Who Follow the Crops. California Governor's Advisory Committee on Children and Youth, Sacramento, 1962.

Williams, Vinnie, *The Fruit Tramp.* New York: Harper & Brothers, 1957.

Work Inquiries in New York State Agriculture. New York State Department of Labor, Albany, 1961.

Working with Migrant Children in Our Schools. Florida State Department of Education, Tallahassee, and the Palm Beach County Public Schools, West Palm Beach. Mimeographed, undated.

Articles

Andrews, John William, "U.S. vs. A&P, Battle of Titans." *Harper's* (September 1950).

Bagdikan, Ben H., "The Invisible Americans." *Saturday Evening Post* (December 21–28, 1963).

"The Glades Side of the Story." The Palm Beach *Post and Times,* Special Supplement (February 8, 1961).

Higbee, Edward, "Now the Non-Farmer Asks for Parity." The *New York Times Sunday Magazine* (June 2, 1963).

Panger, Daniel, "The Forgotten Ones." *The Progressive,* Madison, Wisc. (April 1963).

Manchester, Harland, "Radiation is Producing Better Vegetables," THINK (IBM) (September 1963).

Wright, Dale, "The Forgotten People." Series of articles in the New York *World Telegram & Sun* (October 10–24, 1961).

U.S. Government Printing Office, Washington, D. C.

Agricultural Statistics, 1962. U.S. Department of Agriculture, 1963.

The Community Meets the Migrant Worker. Bulletin 211, U.S. Department of Labor, 1960.

Education and Earnings of the Hired Farm Working Force of 1960. U.S. Department of Agriculture, Economic Research Service, May 1962.

The Education of Migrant Children. U.S. Department of Health, Education and Welfare, 1962.

Farm Labor Fact Book. U.S. Department of Labor, 1959.

Farmers in a Changing World, Yearbook of Agriculture, 1940. U.S. Department of Agriculture, 1940.

The Hired Farm Working Force of 1960. U.S. Department of Agriculture, Economic Research Service, July 1962.

Housing for Farm Labor. Committee on Banking and Currency, May 31 and June 1, 1961.

Housing for Florida's Migrants. U.S. Department of Labor and Florida Industrial Commission, August 1958.

Housing for Migrant Agricultural Workers. Bulletin 235, U.S. Department of Labor, November 1961.

The Impact of Technological Change on Marketing Costs and Grower's Returns. Report 573, U.S. Department of Agriculture, Economic Research Service, 1963.

Information Concerning Entry of Mexican Agricultural Workers into the United States. Bureau of Employment Security, Farm Placement Service, 1957.

Marketing, Yearbook of Agriculture, 1954. U.S. Department of Agriculture, 1954.

Mexican Farm Labor Program (mimeographed). Employment Security Commission, Consultants Report, 1959.

The Migratory Farm Labor Problem in the United States. Senate hearings. Report 1098, September 20, 1961.

The Migratory Farm Labor Problem in the United States. Senate hearings. Report 1225, 1962.

Migratory Labor. Hearings before the Subcommittee on Migratory Labor. Committee on Labor and Public Welfare. S 3382, Volume 3, 1963.

Migratory Labor in American Agriculture. Report of the President's Commission on Migratory Labor, 1951.

Migratory Labor Notes. President's Commission on Migratory Labor (issued irregularly).

National Organizations for Migrant Farm Workers and Their Families. U.S. Department of Labor. Bulletin 236, December 1961.

Problems Involved in Applying a Federal Minimum Wage to Agricultural Workers (two volumes). U.S. Department of Labor, April 30, 1960.

Selected References on Domestic Agricultural Workers, 1955–1960. U.S. Department of Labor. Bulletin 225, 1961.

Selected References on Migrant Education. U.S. Department of Health, Education and Welfare, February 1963.

Small Business Problems in the Poultry Industry. House Report 2566, 1963.

Small Business Problems in the Tomato Industry. House Report 1471, 1962.

State Migratory Labor Committees, Their Organization and Programs. U.S. Department of Labor. Bulletin 215, 1960.

Underhill Ruth, *Here Comes the Navaho.* U.S. Department of Interior, 1953.

Yearbook of the Department of Agriculture. U.S. Department of Agriculture, 1906.

INDEX

About the Author

TRUMAN MOORE was born on a small farm in Georgia. He spent most of his childhood on a farm in Tennessee, and later the family moved to South Carolina.

He graduated from the University of North Carolina in 1957. He now lives in New York City, where he is a writer and a photographer. His photographs have appeared in *Life* and other national magazines. This is his first book.